Signs of Grace

Signs of Grace

Meditations on the Notre Dame Campus

Father Nicholas Ayo, C.S.C.

ROWMAN & LITTLEFIELD PUBLISHERS, INC.
Lanham • Boulder • New York • Plymouth, UK

ROWMAN & LITTLEFIELD PUBLISHERS, INC.

Published in the United States of America
by Rowman & Littlefield Publishers, Inc.
A wholly owned subsidiary of The Rowman & Littlefield Publishing Group, Inc.
4501 Forbes Boulevard, Suite 200, Lanham, Maryland 20706
www.rowmanlittlefield.com

Estover Road
Plymouth PL6 7PY
United Kingdom

First paperback edition 2007

British Library Cataloguing in Publication Information Available

The hardback edition of this book was previously cataloged by the Library of Congress as follows:

Ayo, Nicholas.
Signs of grace : meditations on the Notre Dame campus / Nicholas Ayo.
p. cm.
ISBN-13: 978-0-7425-2189-6 (cloth : alk. paper)
ISBN-10: 0-7425-2189-3 (cloth : alk. paper)
ISBN-13: 978-0-7425-4829-9 (pbk. : alk. paper)
ISBN-10: 0-7425-4829-5 (pbk. : alk. paper)
1 Meditations. 2. University of Notre Dame. I. Title.

BX2177.A96 2001
242—dc21 2001048622

Printed in the United States of America

∞™ The paper used in this publication meets the minimum requirements of American National Standard for Information Sciences—Permanence of Paper for Printed Library Materials, ANSI/NISO Z39.48-1992.

DEDICATED TO

Father Theodore Martin Hesburgh, C.S.C.,

the Second Founder of the University of Notre Dame

Contents

Foreword

ONE OF MY responsibilities as president of the University of Notre Dame is to attempt to describe in various ways the enduring sense of attractiveness of the campus itself. The physical terrain, the two lakes, the Grotto, the trees and flowers and grass, the statuary, the most recognizable buildings—like the Main Building, the Basilica, the football stadium, the Hesburgh Library—are the backdrop, the context within which the experience of the institution in all of its complexity takes place. For those who have attended the university or worked at it or visited it frequently, each of the special places can have particular memories attached. Students recall the dorms within which they have lived, the classrooms and laboratories they haunted, the libraries within which they did research, and the interior and exterior spaces where they engaged in extracurricular activities of every sort. Like lovers and friends who can have deep memories recalled by hearing a song or visiting a special place, so the people of Notre Dame often find in the beauty of the campus and in the sweep of its quads and various outdoor spaces stimulation for reflection about the passing of the seasons and the stages of life.

One of my favorite images of Notre Dame is that it has become a place of pilgrimage for those who have lived here in the past as well as those who have related to the university but never had the experience of first-hand participation. On home football weekends, with the press of thousands of visitors, many come early and leave late. In a sense, the game is an excuse for a fuller experience of campus life and a chance to renew friendships and reflect with one's family and friends about the special nature of the place and the memories it evokes. On alumni reunion weekends, this sort of encounter with the past is magnified many fold. You see graduates of every age group sitting quietly on one of the many benches spread around the campus to have a chance to think, to reflect, and to pray. For those who are here on a full-time basis, there is nothing more rejuvenating than a meditative walk around the lakes or a prayerful visit at the Grotto.

A significant dimension of Notre Dame as a center of pilgrimage is the way we have preserved the traditional parts of the campus while still moving forward in response to new opportunities for academic, social, and athletic improvement. In a fast-paced world where often the memories of one's youth have been destroyed or rendered unfamiliar, Notre Dame remains a familiar place with a plethora of places and sight lines prized by successive generations of its faculty, staff, and students.

Father Ayo's wonderful book is a perfect aid to memory and a stimulus to our inner need for peaceful musing and heartfelt recall. With the insight of a poet/theologian, he offers us brief but incisive insights into multiple campus locations. Whether used directly for an actual reflective walk around the campus or more vicariously at a distance, this book opens up new possibilities for comprehending how beauty and meaning are essential needs of the human person.

I recommend this work to you with deep conviction that your journey to Notre Dame will be guided well toward the transformation of self that is the wonderful result of encounters with places that are holy.

Rev. Edward A. Malloy, C.S.C.
Former President of the University of Notre Dame

Prologue

MASS IN THE Basilica of the Sacred Heart on a Sunday morning is always crowded with visitors as well as the usual campus and parish regulars. Especially on football weekends one must come early to find a place, and people are often turned away at the doors because the Basilica is overflowing and the aisles are crowded with standees. No one finds it a familiar routine to attend church on a football weekend. But here they are in huge numbers, and I think I know why.

We all need a dream. We cannot live without a dream. We want our story, the story of our life, to be part of a larger story. We cannot live without meaning, and our own life in isolation has no compelling purpose. In the contemporary world people do not often find a bigger meaning in their employment. They work for a large company, perhaps, but they are not needed for who they are in their unique identity. Someone else could take their place. They do not feel part of a bigger picture and a meaningful outcome. Those people who lived through World War II reminisce about the sense of common purpose they experienced in those troubled years. There was a mission and a goal. There was a common endeavor, and one felt a needed member of a team where everyone's efforts were needed and appreciated. Life for the individual was part of the story of life for the country. We belonged to each other in a way that gave a sense of a dream shared and pursued in community. We would together make a better world, a world fit for human beings, a world of freedom and no more war. It was like the excitement that the disciples of Jesus must have known when they were engaged in bringing about the Kingdom of God on Earth. It was mission; it was vocation; it was a communion of saints.

At Notre Dame the Congregation of Holy Cross provides a sense of the larger purpose of our lives. We all are working together as a community for the building of the Kingdom of God. There is a deep sense of camaraderie in this endeavor and an appreciation for the various and diverse gifts of others. In the religious life it is clear that we enjoy a garden where many flowers can bloom. No one is left out, and everyone contributes. Some people have high-profile lives and enjoy success in the eyes of the world, and others lead a more hidden life in Nazareth. No one is unneeded, and at our best we bear one another's burdens. What happens in a concentrated and public way in a religious congregation should also be experienced by every baptized person in the church community to which they belong. We all work for the coming of the Kingdom of God. We all say in the Lord's Prayer "thy Kingdom come." The focus of this, our life's endeavor, seems easily blurred in the day-to-day confusion of life in the world and our own preoccupation with consumption and flight from the reality of our death. Our only true need, however, remains the grace of God. That is why Sunday mass in the Basilica of Notre Dame has such impact. Here and now the people in the congregation feel part of the people of God in this larger dream. Somehow the Kingdom of God can be glimpsed in the raising up of a university dedicated to the promotion of God's truth and God's love. Not that everyone at Notre Dame is a saint, nor that everyone in the Basilica is holy, nor that all the baptized whether by water, or fire, or desire in the whole worldwide Catholic Church is filled with the grace of God; but what is true is that for a moment one sees and feels what it might be like were the grace of God to spread its wonders in all our lives all the time.

Blaise Pascal, the brilliant mathematician and spiritual seeker of seventeenth-century France, is often remembered for a wager that he suggested to anyone whose faith was weak and who did not greatly care to lead the Christian life. Pascal argued that one cannot live without some kind of purpose, some kind of dream, some kind of discipline. Without meaning our life is chaos. Thus Pascal concludes: choose to lead a Christian life and you will have meaning and purpose. Your life will be disciplined and you will find happiness in the virtues of Christianity that are often their own reward. Take a chance on God. Should it turn out at death there is no God and nothing more, you will know no pain and you will have led a fruitful and peaceful life in this world. Should it turn out at death there is a God whose kingdom will never end, then you will have won the wager and attained everlasting life and endless happiness. Not exactly full faith, but "Lord, help thou my unbelief."

Carved over the portal of the east entrance to the transept of the Basilica are the words "God, Country, Notre Dame." On the sides of the portal are the names of those Notre Dame graduates who lost their lives in World War I. They knew the larger purpose, and they had a faith to die for. But so do we all have a faith to die for and a faith to live for. We are all called to lay down our lives for our friends, to give our lives in service and in love for the Kingdom of God. Visitors to Notre Dame who come to the Basilica for Sunday mass are reminded that the Kingdom of God is found in our country as Jesus was found in Bethlehem, where one would least have looked for God, in the place where the animals were sheltered. And the Kingdom of God is found in Notre Dame as Jesus was found in Nazareth, in the hidden life waiting for the mission that led to the cross, the resurrection into eternal life, and the salvation of the world. Here is Christian life "under the Dome."

Acknowledgments

MANY PEOPLE HAVE generously assisted me in this endeavor. Alida Macor, Kathleen Karras, and Father Leonard Banas, C.S.C., read the manuscript in various stages and made helpful suggestions that were followed. Fathers William Seetch, C.S.C., John Jenkins, C.S.C., and Edward Malloy, C.S.C., were instrumental in the promotion of this project. My student assistants, Emily Reimer and Brian Casas, proofread the manuscript as well as investigated particular questions of information. Professor Doris Watt at Saint Mary's College was helpful. Robert Hamma at Ave Maria Press and the Alumni Association gave consideration to the manuscript. Without James Langford, editor for Rowman & Littlefield, this text would not have been published. I am most indebted to his recognition of the potential of these campus reflections. His eager promotion of its publication has made all the difference. My nephew, John Macor, provided the photograph used as the cover illustration. The support of the Congregation of Holy Cross, the Program of Liberal Studies, and the University of Notre Dame is so constant as to be unnoticed, but it is not taken for granted. I remain grateful and beholden to all these people and others unmentioned, whose contributions I may have forgotten or overlooked. "No man is an island" is a wisdom well understood by authors.

Starting Places

The Visitors' Center and the Bookstore

The Visitation of Mary and Elizabeth

Brother André, C.S.C.

Christ the Teacher

Morning Prayer

The Visitors' Center and the Bookstore

FIRST-TIME VISITORS to the campus linger in a friendly building complex off Notre Dame Avenue at the entrance to the university. The Alumni Association has its offices in a beautiful welcome-center of Gothic design adjacent to the bookstore. Marble floors and magnificent cherry woodwork crafted by Amish artisans throughout the Eck Center (Visitors' Center and Hammes Bookstore) lift the spirit as one wanders the large open spaces of both buildings. Beauty used to be a luxury the university could hardly afford.

Even in the old bookstore, people complained about high prices. Clothing with the Notre Dame logo are quality goods at corresponding cost. And in the end, the secret of peace of mind in the Notre Dame check-out line is to consider one's tab as a donation to the university. One can be concerned that we have too much materialism in our spiritual lives. Are we wealthy people who happen to be spiritual, or are we a spiritual people first who happen to be wealthy. We are stewards of the wealth of this world, whether that wealth is what is sold in a bookstore or taught in a classroom. We do not own what is given us and never was ours; we are given to be caretakers of our gifts and the things of this world. The student initiatives to promote fair labor practices in the manufacturing of the logo-clothing sold in the bookstore seemed to me a sign of our spiritual life confronting the vicissitudes of commercial life and championing justice.

The Notre Dame bookstore carries a wide range of publications. Course books for students are distributed. Books published by the University of Notre Dame Press, Ave Maria Press, and faculty members are featured, as well as a judicious selection of all fields of intellectual concern at a university. A cozy reading area invites browsing. Gift books, religious articles, clothing, fine crystal, class rings, memorabilia, and souvenirs of Notre Dame also abound. In French, *souvenir* means to remember. In the splendor of this magnificent bookstore I want to remember that Notre Dame was once very poor, that American Catholics were once immigrants in the main, and that our forebears suffered persecution and discrimination. Whenever the day comes that we do not remember our historical roots, our origin in God, and the providence that has blessed us and delivered us from so many enslavements will be the day that the bookstore becomes the mirror of our decline. What Notre Dame does best is the celebration of the eucharist "in memory of Him." The good thief on Calvary hill asked Jesus "to remember him when he came into his kingdom" (Lk 23:42). Lest we forget! The goods and riches of the earth are God's gifts, and if we take them home as God's souvenirs and Notre Dame souvenirs as well, then all will be well. Riches are not evil, but to be a good and faithful steward of riches is an ever-demanding challenge.

The Visitors' Center houses the Alumni Association. No university boasts more loyal and more generous graduates than Notre Dame. Reunions on campus bring graduates back in large numbers every summer. Alumni clubs and their "Notre Dame nights" can be enjoyed in every state and many countries in the world. Summer service projects funded by the clubs and engaging current students are a credit to the very mission of the university.

In the Visitors' Center one will find comfort and hospitality, together with an information desk, maps, photographs, and an orientation video film in the auditorium. Here is the place to start a campus tour complete with student guide. These enthusiastic young men and women have been well instructed in Notre Dame lore and legend. You will hear about the ghost of George Gipp still roaming Washington Hall at night and fair-catch Corby on the lawn in front of Corby Hall. But, if you listen carefully, you will hear what no visitor can ever know as the students know. You will hear them speak of their residence hall, of the dorm where they have made lifetime friends and learned so very much of mind, heart, and soul from each other. The alums come back to campus, not so much to visit their teachers as to see their rectors, who knew them twenty-four hours a day, through thick and thin, in times of trouble and family grief, in the painful incidents of their social and spiritual lives. To live at Notre Dame is to come to love Notre Dame. The secret of campus life remains in its people living together on a residential campus, where the individual person is known by name and their whole life in its intellectual, emotional, social, and spiritual dimensions is appreciated. If you want the spirit of Notre Dame, one can begin with the Visitors' Center and end with the souvenirs of the bookstore, but hear what the students love about the University of Notre Dame and its unique community life.

The Visitation of Mary and Elizabeth

BETWEEN THE VISITORS' Center and the Notre Dame bookstore an imposing sculpture welcomes the stranger to the campus of Notre Dame. Two women embrace. Their garments enfold them like a protective tent. Both women are ample and one might well suspect they are both large with child. Their bodies touch where their children lie hidden. They lean forward to caress each other's face. The hands of the older woman encircle the waist of the younger woman, and she holds onto the broad shoulders of her cousin Elizabeth. The gospel story of the visitation of Mary of Nazareth to Elizabeth of Jerusalem comes to life in the bronze artwork of the beloved Notre Dame sculptor, Reverend Anthony (Tony) Lauck, C.S.C.

The meeting of these two women is a fitting introduction to Notre Dame. Our Lady (Notre Dame), the mother of Jesus and the mother of God, greets an old and tired world awaiting its light and its salvation in the coming generation. Mary carries within her a miracle child, for she was "too young" (yet unmarried and a virgin) to conceive a child. Elizabeth's child is also a miracle child, as we read in Luke's gospel account (1:39–80). Beyond childbearing years she was "too old," yet she continued to pray to God for new life. The grace of God is limited neither by circumstance nor age, for God's creative love is ever sovereign. An angel of the Lord appears in the Temple to Elizabeth's husband, Zachary, who is offering sacrifice in the Holy of Holies. Gabriel announces the coming birth of a son, whose name would be John. Zachary is skeptical that his wife could possibly conceive a child in her old age; therefore, he must learn to listen and to await in faith God's graceful initiative. Struck speechless, he can only look upon the surprising mystery of God's visitation. Elizabeth, however, knows she is a vessel of God's creative love, and when she embraces her cousin, who has traveled from her home to be with Elizabeth in her sixth month, she recognizes the Christ in Mary and exclaims "And why has this happened to me, that the mother of my Lord comes to me?" (Lk 1:43) Even the unborn John, who would become the herald of Jesus, recognizes the divine visitation. The gospel tells that he leapt with joy to greet his Lord yet unborn in his mother Mary's womb.

Upon reflection one can see how fitting it is to greet the visitor to Notre Dame, whether newcomer or oldcomer, with this poignant reminder of the visitation of Mary and Elizabeth. We too should recognize Christ Jesus in one another and embrace those given us, young and old, with the love we give our incarnate Lord. We bring Christ to each other. The cathedral architecture of the Eck Visitors' Center and the Hammes Bookstore might easily remind us all of our dignity as human beings. "Do you not know that you are God's temple and that God's Spirit dwells in you?" (1 Cor 3:16).

In the Visitation story the old world of Israel, always the chosen people of a faithful God, meets the new world of its fulfillment in Jesus Christ. The new and old embrace each other. Incarnate revelation embraces the world. The old is asked to change, not to be undone but in order to remain its true self. When Notre Dame University admitted undergraduate women in 1972, it was a change, but one that was asked of us in order to stay the same. The university's mission always was then and always will be to school the coming leaders of our society with the best possible education informed by the truths of the gospel. When leadership roles of many kinds became newly accessible to women, Notre Dame could but gratefully and graciously welcome them to its student body. The Visitation sculpture at this entrance of the university reminds the visitor and the resident of what we are truly here to recognize and accomplish.

Brother André, C.S.C.

HIGH ON THE south wall of the Visitors' Center, facing the visitor to the Notre Dame campus approaching from the parking area stands a life-size statue of Blessed Brother André, C.S.C. He was a man small in stature but large in heart. André Bessette was a Holy Cross brother who spent his life as a humble doorkeeper, who in his own way led a multitude to Saint Joseph. He stands even now at the door to Notre Dame as he stood at the door greeting visitors to the Holy Cross Middle School in Montreal, Canada. His hand is outstretched with palm up as if presenting us whatever is needed. What can Notre Dame give you? Whom have you come to find? What do you seek in this place?

In his arms he carries a lily, symbol of Saint Joseph in his single-hearted love for God. In his hand he holds a key ring. "Listen, I am standing at the door knocking; if you hear my voice and open the door, I will come in to you and eat with you, and you with me" (Rv 3:20). It was Saint Benedict who taught the Western world that the stranger should be greeted as if they were Christ knocking at our door. Indeed, we do greet Christ in the visitor, for "just as you did to one of the least of these who are members of my family, you did it to me" (Mt 25:40).

At Brother André's feet there is a stone carving of the Oratory of Saint Joseph, the magnificent shrine built to accommodate the growing devotion to Saint Joseph that Brother

André initiated with the smallest endeavors. With compassionate heart he would listen to visitors at the door while they awaited the person summoned to meet them. André heard the troubles of the world; he knew the misery of the little people who had nowhere else to turn for help. He would give them a medal of Saint Joseph and a printed card with a prayer to Saint Joseph and some oil blessed with prayers to Saint Joseph. Christians are a sacramental people, and these shy tokens were what people in dire need could cling to for hope and consolation. A small chapel was built by volunteers, and then enlarged, and then more people came, and in the end the shrine of Saint Joseph would comfort a world in its carrying of the cross of Jesus. "Go to Joseph!" echo the words of Jacob in time of famine when his son Joseph, then thought to be dead, was in charge of the grain reserves in Egypt. In God's providence Joseph would feed God's people.

Visitors come to Notre Dame in SUVs, in vans, in campers, and in vehicles of every description. No matter how we arrive, we are all fellow pilgrims, fellow travelers, nomads on planet Earth, having here no lasting home, only stopping by to visit en route to our home in heaven. Notre Dame wishes to welcome everyone with Blessed Brother André. We would be mindful that the stranger, the alien, the unborn, the widow, the helpless, the poor and the rich, and all this multitude of humanity most of all needs to be made at home. Notre Dame aspires to be a catholic (universal) university. Together everyone who visits this campus makes up the extended family of Notre Dame (Our Lady, mother of God). We hope to recognize in each other the dearly beloved children of God, our sisters and brothers, the people of God, who are the living stones of the new Jerusalem.

Christ the Teacher

JUST NORTH OF the bookstore, on the path to the heart of the campus, the visitor will see the figure of Jesus sitting on a hard rock on an open hillside facing the golden dome and the Basilica of the Sacred Heart in the distance. The bronze sculpture was a gift of the class of 2000, dedicated "in honor of Catholic education in the new millennium" and presented "in thanksgiving for lessons learned in heart and mind." Inscribed on the plaque are also words about Jesus Christ the teacher found in the Gospel of John: "All the people came to him, and he sat down and began to teach them" (8:2).

There is another depiction of Christ the teacher that in size and impressiveness dwarfs this small sculpture so quietly resting under the shade of an oak tree in the middle of an empty field. The image of Christ is enormous and fills the south wall of the Hesburgh Library. Surrounding him one sees the many and varied figures through the centuries who were teachers in the prefiguration and in the imitation of Christ. Encircling the reflecting pool at the base of this mosaic mural, low marble walls name the many endowed chairs at the university. From their established seat of authority distinguished professors teach the students who come to sit at their feet. With the generous growth of the endowments of these prestigious chairs in all the branches of learning at the university, one hears humorous talk of overstuffed chairs, now large enough to fund more than one professor in any given "chair." In contrast, Jesus taught as he went from place to place. He had no place to lay his head in his earthly life. Despite his poverty, however, the ultimate chairholder at the University of Notre Dame now sits on a more than generously endowed chair at the right hand of the Father in heaven, "from whence he will come to judge the living and the dead." His gospel truth will not pass away, because it is founded not on sand nor writ in marble stone, but spoken by the Lord God whose word is the rock of ages.

Saint Benedict says in his *Rule* that the monastery community should always listen to the voice of their youngest member, for the Holy Spirit of God might choose to speak through the least of the brethren. Christ the teacher seated on a bare rock is a reminder to us all who dwell at this university or visit its grounds that we should revere the young people entrusted to us and not only teach them. When the disciples wanted to keep Jesus from wasting his time with the young who hardly counted in their society, Jesus rebukes them. "'Let the little children come to me; do not stop them; for it is to such as these that the kingdom of God belongs. Truly I tell you, whoever does not receive the kingdom of God as a little child will never enter it.' And he took them up in his arms, laid his hands on them, and blessed them" (Mk 10:14–16).

Jesus sits under a tree on the land that for so many years was part of the Notre Dame golf course. The scene is pastoral and innocent. He holds out his closed right hand with two fingers extended in a blessing and as if emphasizing whether it was point one or point two of his exposition of the matter at hand. Worrisome this scene is not. But we might remember that the endeavor to teach the students that come to Notre Dame includes an awesome responsibility. Our students are entrusted to the university, and they remain in the hands and in the care of their teachers at a time in their lives when they are most impressionable and most willing to be inspired. To lead them astray by word or by example, to fail to be mentors and imitators of Christ-like love in their lives, to give scandal or take advantage of their innocence and vulnerability deserves more than criticism. Jesus was passionate about guarding the idealism and generosity of the young. "If any of you put a stumbling block before one of these little ones who believe in me, it would be better for you if a great millstone were hung around your neck and you were thrown into the sea" (Mk 9:42).

Morning Prayer

IN THE EARLY morning before sunrise on Thanksgiving Day, I am sitting on the swinging bench on the porch of Sorin Hall, or Sorin College as the residents love to call it from its early days as the first residence hall of the university (the dormitories until then had all been in the Main Building). Knute Rockne lived in Sorin College. It was founded at the time of the fiftieth anniversary of Father Sorin's ordination to the priesthood, the same time that the Grotto was built. Here was history. But I was sitting on a cloudy Thanksgiving Day with only a sliver of clear sky near the horizon in the east, hoping against hope that I would see a beautiful sunrise to be thankful for. Yet I know morning prayer is much more prosaic. The clouds were not going to allow the sun to sparkle or the colors of the rainbow to emerge. The light was there, and the sun would rise, of course, as a matter of course. And that was the thanksgiving of each morning of every day. That the sun rises, that we are alive on planet Earth, that God is in God's heaven and we are the beloved of our creator. Our last thanksgiving day would be everlasting and we would sit in the full light of God, beyond any beauty these eyes could comprehend on this Earth.

On this morning the only sound came from flocks of crows. Every morning as I hope for a sunrise and give thanks for the light no matter the clouds, I hear the cawing of the crows. Today all else is quiet. There are no delivery trucks, no early maintenance trucks, no predawn construction crews revving up the diesel engines of their cranes and dozers, no students slamming the front door as they run late to their breakfast or their job in the dining hall. Just the quiet, the gray sky, and the cawing of dozens of crows. They fly around in disturbed circles, the mild panic of one bird setting off the flight of its neighbor. Their voices are strident, and their reputation as scavengers and nest robbers gives them a sinister quality. To look at their purple-black glossy feathers is to see a dark beauty. They fly with an agility that is wondrous given their size. They seem to me hawks that never became proud of being a raptor. I once saw a crow with a baby rabbit in its beak. It flew to the roof of the building, with the sparrows and starlings who had seen its crib robbery in hot pursuit and vociferous complaint. They knew one could never trust a crow. They were harbingers of death.

When I was very young we had a servant who came once a week to help my mother clean our home. Her name was Ella, and she knew tragedy in her own family a-plenty. She used to say, in the acceptance that her faith in God lent her, that "we are born to die." I still recall those words, and I know they are true. That death is part of life is not meant to be sad. That night and day overlap is what I know when I wait for the sunrise in the dark. "We are born to die." Maybe the black crows that live as scavengers are a reminder of our mortality, that nothing lasts forever, that no one but God has life everlasting within. Be that as it may, when I hear the crows and watch the skies for the coming of the light, I know that the substance of every morning prayer remains. I am alive this morning, and God watches us with power and love every night. God's light rises with the sun every morning to shine in our hearts that know and love him and are given yet this day to sing God's praises that we were born to die and promised to live forever in the mystical body of Our Lord Jesus Christ.

Sacred Places

The Dome at Night

Joyce Center Mass

The Grotto

The Threshold of God's House

The Splendor of the Basilica

Christian Death

The Steeple Bells

Weddings and Baptisms

Calvary Hill

God's Acre

The Dome at Night

THE GOLDEN DOME at Notre Dame shines brightly in the sunshine against a deep blue sky. There are days when to look up at Mary on the Dome is to have one's breath taken away. The whole scene is so glorious—gold, blue, sky, clouds, and a fresh breeze. One is breathing grace and not just clear air. The university gilds the Dome every so many years to keep it brilliant, and fine gold leaf is appliquéd. The cost stems not so much from the fine gold as from the labor to erect scaffolding and the skilled craftsman who must work at a height. Were Notre Dame ever to lack the money to gild the Dome, I would do without a meal a day to donate. Even poor people find enough money to buy a small wedding ring of gold. And the Dome is how this university community shows its love for the spouse of us all, the Holy Spirit of God who came to dwell in the body of Mary of Nazareth, who birthed Jesus the Christ into our world, and who is ever the mother of God and our mother, Notre Dame.

Splendid as the Dome may be by day, it is at night, against a blackened sky that it shines with most brilliance. In all kinds of weather, whatever the hour or the day, the Dome is illuminated as the light of faith in a world of darkness. "A great portent appeared in heaven: a woman clothed with the sun, with the moon under her feet, and on her head a crown of twelve stars" (Rv 12:1). Approaching the university by plane in the evening hours, the Dome is a guidepost not only for the pilot but also for the traveler, heart-weary away from home. Coming back from Chicago on the Tollway there is a rise in the road when suddenly and briefly the Dome can be seen in the distance. It is a most welcome sight in the late hours of the night, for we travel through this vale of tears always on the way to our heavenly home and guided by her who is "our life, our sweetness, and our hope."

Outside the windows of the rooms where I live I look upon the Basilica of the Sacred Heart aside my residence. Just beyond the church, the golden Dome rises high into the blue skies. In the evening the gold-leafed statue of our Lady is bathed in the warm beams of floodlights. The entire Dome surface shimmers underneath her feet and the stars sparkle in the dark night sky above her head. On a summer night as I sat looking out the window at the Basilica, that house of God, and the gleaming Dome in the evening sky rising above her, I watched in fascination the aerial display of the diving nighthawks on all sides. Their agility is so beautiful to watch. They turn without warning and seemingly beyond the possible. The wing is faster than the eye. The mastery of flight is breathtaking, for the birds swoop out of darkness, speed through the light, and disappear almost as the sounding notes of a song come and go.

And yet there are shadows even in the flood of these golden lights. The moths and mosquitoes attracted to the light they cannot but love are cut down in the killing fields where their prey ambush them and take their life when caught in the glare that blinds and dizzies them. No one intends harm in this scene. It is not the Dome maker's fault, or the light that shines as a beacon in the night, nor the nighthawks that must eat, nor the insects (God's lowly creatures) that must die all the while in the light and striving with all their might to reach our Lady's feet. We are born to die, and the woman on the Dome is the same woman who held the crucified body of her dead son on her lap. *Per aspera ad astra* (through rough times to the stars) was an ancient proverb, and the gospel equivalent might be "unless you lose your life you shall not find it."

When our Blessed Mother at the end of her life fell asleep, we believe she was taken up into heaven body and soul, where she is seated with Jesus her son in the heart of the Blessed Trinity. Dante imagines a gigantic white rose filled with light, and the blessed saints seated as in a Greek amphitheater rapt in their joy at the vision of God face to face. No one claims to have buried the bones of this woman. And it would have been a mighty temptation to fabricate a shrine built at the site of a burial. St. Peter's Basilica in Rome is built over his bones. The Church of the Resurrection in Jerusalem is built over the empty tomb of Jesus. But of Mary there are no bones and no tomb. If the wages of sin are death, the wages of innocence must be life. If Mary's body in its purity was the tabernacle of the infinity of God and the dwelling place of the beloved Son of God made flesh in her womb, one cannot imagine that God would allow his mother to decay. She is queen of heaven, the "ark of the covenant," the "mystical rose," the "house of gold," as the litany of Loreto proclaims. No wonder the founders of Notre Dame enthroned her in the heavens crowned upon a golden Dome.

Joyce Center Mass

MOST PEOPLE THINK of the Joyce Center at Notre Dame (the Athletic and Convocation Center) because of basketball season or hockey games. It is a sports arena. On special occasions when the congregation overflows the Basilica, the Eucharist is celebrated here. When the first-year students arrive, the Sunday mass for the almost 2000 students, plus parents, family, and friends of the new Domers, almost fills the basketball arena. I have found these moments ecstatic with happiness, albeit a bittersweet happiness. Good-bye-for-now weighs on the hearts of family members who may never before have lived apart. Hope abounds, nonetheless, and the arena could be christened the Joy Center. You can feel the love of parents for their children. They loved them and raised them through thick and thin to bring them here for this moment. They want them to learn to live their own life. They know to love them truly they must let them go. The mystery of love is always the mystery of the cross. Love requires sacrifice, sooner or later. Love cannot avoid pain and sustain love. We must say good-bye to everything and everyone we love, in due time and in due place. There is no joy without the cross, no eternal life with God in infinite joy without the passage of dying. The Paschal mystery is our life and we live it out in the celebration of Christ's last supper, where he said and lived those words: "this is my body, given up for you." When I was a young boy, one of the poignant spiritual experiences of my life was my first inkling of mortality. I broke my shoelaces, and in a flash I knew in my heart that everything would break, sooner or later. My parents would break, the world would break, I would break. It was a moment of grace that I knew how without God we are nothing.

One of the extraordinary moments in the Joyce Center mass occurs at communion time. The residence hall rectors, who have the pastoral care of these new students at Notre Dame, are Eucharist ministers along with the concelebrating university priests. The congregation is in the thousands, and communion even with organization takes many minutes. I stand on the steps and watch these parents filled with hope, with pride in their children, with anxiety about how they will manage without them, and I want to say more than "the body of Christ." I want to say, "*You are* the body of Christ. *I see you.*" In the Eucharist the bread and wine are changed into the body and blood of Jesus Christ, but it is not God who needs change. In the reception of the Eucharist the greatest miracle of all remains just this. We change. We become the body of Christ. This bread is given for us, not for God. We are the ones who are blessed to become Christ. "You are *the body of Christ.*"

At the close of this mass, the university president asks parents, family, and friends to stand and hold their hands outstretched in the recitation of a communal blessing upon all these first-year students whom they have brought to this point of independence in their life. It is a poignant moment, and tears flow easily. These faithful, loving people have brought today to this Eucharist the bread and wine. It is their sons and daughters to be changed, to be changed into the body of Christ, to become the Church, to become closer to God, whatever their declared religion may prove to be. Mass stipends are not as customary as some years ago, but what a stipend means is this: If you bring the bread and wine, your share in this Eucharist is unique. Better yet, grow the wheat and grapes and make the bread and make the wine. But, lacking that opportunity, a small donation allows the priest to purchase them. But best of all, bread and wine is the son or daughter that you present to God, and whom you made from your own body and raised with your own hands and gave spiritual life to with your own heart's blood, and to whom you must now say for the nonce "good-bye, God be with you."

The Grotto

THE NOTRE DAME Grotto, nestled in the wooded hillside between the Basilica and Saint Mary's Lake, is a replica of the grotto of Lourdes in France, where the mother of Jesus appeared to Bernadette Soubirous in 1845 and revealed to her the mystery of the Immaculate Conception. Mary was conceived without sin, which is the foreshadowing of and preparation for the greater mystery of the virginal conception of Jesus and the incarnation of the Word of God in her womb.

Many are the stories about the Grotto at Notre Dame.[1] I have often wanted to spend an uninterrupted twenty-four hours sitting there and watching what happens. I do not think one would be alone. There seems always to be someone coming and someone going in the Grotto. Even late at night, the people who are night owls pay a visit to the Grotto to say a night prayer. And it would not be long before those who are morning doves pay a visit to the Grotto to say a morning prayer. No one teaches the students and the family of Notre Dame about the Grotto in a formal way. One observes others at the Grotto, and the tradition that here is a sacred place, a place belonging to our Lady, Notre Dame, becomes ingrained in everyone who lives here. I have seen people just sitting still in the Grotto. I have seen

1. See *Stories about the Grotto*. Published by the Alumni Association of Notre Dame and available in the Notre Dame Bookstore.

animated conversation in the Grotto. I have seen lovers arm in arm on the benches surrounding the Grotto. I have seen young and old on their knees at the railing. There are masses held in the Grotto. And the rosary every evening. The water in the fountain bubbles up without fail in the warm weather. Brides beautify the grounds as they pose in our Lady's shadow to take their wedding pictures. Flowers are planted, and bouquets are left here and there by the devotion of someone unknown. The candles burn constantly by the hundreds, day and night, every day of the year. It is a perpetual flame, a prayer from Notre Dame to *Notre Dame* that never ends.

One evening the Grotto caught fire. A student called the fire department at the university and said that the Grotto was on fire. But no one there took the report seriously. It sounded like a student prank, like reporting that the lake was on fire. But the Grotto *was* on fire. The week-long candles had been purchased in plastic containers rather than glass containers, and on a busy football weekend there were hundreds of these candles burning. The combined heat around and underneath the plastic containers ignited a conflagration. All the wax went up in flames. The pink dogwood planted on top of the Grotto hillside was singed. The stones were blackened but not burned. All was eventually restored, and another grace was revealed. If one has faith to see the glory of Mary, the Grotto is always on fire. One has but to believe in order to see.

Tom Dooley's statue off to the side of the Grotto apron and hidden in the trees shows him with the children of Vietnam to whom he ministered with medicine and with love as a Navy doctor during the Vietnam War. When dying young of cancer, he wrote to Father Hesburgh telling of his devotion to the Grotto and his longing to be there now, even when he was so far away. The letter lies etched in a bronze plaque before the memorial statue. As much as one admires Dr. Dooley, we know it is not we the people who were conceived without sin. It is only she who is "our tainted nature's solitary boast," and to seek her company is to desire the mercy and grace of her son, Our Lord, Jesus Christ.

At Christmas time the crib scene is displayed on the Grotto lawns. One year someone stole the baby Jesus from the straw in the middle of the night. They later wanted a ransom. One does not know whether to laugh or cry. But I was reminded of the story in the gospel of the weeds and the wheat. Good and evil exist in this world side by side with their roots entangled. It is not easy here and now to separate sin and grace, for the human heart is the soil for both. And yet one surely knows in the Grotto as no where else that where sin abounded grace did abound the more.

Time passes at the Grotto, but the Grotto perdures. I remember feeling heartsick when the diseased Dutch elms, once so widely beautiful, were cut down. New trees will come. When Father Joyce and Father Hesburgh retired together in the mid-1980s, in their honor they planted a pink dogwood for Father Ned and a contorted filbert for Father Ted, on whom the humor was not lost. I like to go to the Grotto to pray and to smile, as I imagine our Lady smiles down on us. Trust God, and be at peace. The Lord who made the universe became a little child in a woman's arms, died on a cross, but now sits in glory at the right hand of the Father Almighty. *Hail Mary, full of grace, the Lord is with thee, blessed are thou among women and blessed is the fruit of thy womb, Jesus.*

The Threshold of God's House

GOING THROUGH A doorway from a world outside to a world inside is always an adventure. From the campus whirl outside into the inside of the Basilica at Notre Dame does give one pause. A vast space opens up with high ceilings and gold decorations on soaring pillars. Stained glass windows turn even the colors of earth and sky more rich in their diversity. And into that world we must come through a narrow door. As the stonework on the facade begins to channel us into the church, we are drawn to cross a threshold.

In the gospel Jesus describes himself as the door of the sheepfold. In the fenced enclosure where the sheep are sleeping, Jesus himself lays his body down on the threshold as the protector of the sheep from the dangers of the night. His life would be given up for theirs. I once perused the blueprint of a medieval monastery. Among the outbuildings there was a residence for any visiting knight who might be traveling by. The paddock for his horse was attached to the back of the one-room house. But there was no door into the paddock. Suddenly I understood. The knight's horse was valuable just as a Porsche sports car might be to us today. The only way to steal the horse was to bring it out through the front door of the house and over the sleeping body of the knight himself. We have the saying "over my dead body," and it sounds a note of commitment.

Once through the massive carved wooden doors of the Basilica, one stands underneath the many bells of the steeple tower and in the foyer of the church. A stained glass window depicting the souls of the dead in the fires of purgatory reminds one that here is the anteroom of heaven. Then one passes into the nave of the Basilica underneath an archway whose symbolism deserves attention. Carved in the glasswork are the letters alpha and omega, the first and the last letters of the Greek alphabet. It is Jesus who from birth to death, from first to last, is our Lord and Savior. The Greek letters that abbreviate the word Jesus (IHS) are also carved there, as is the symbol of the cross. No more need be said. It is through the mystery of the love of God revealed in the cross of Jesus Christ that we are from the beginning of the world to its ending within the mystery of divine love.

The nave of the church is so named from the Latin word for boat *(navis)*, and in imagination the church nave is a long boat—the ark of Noah in the flood, our safety in the storm at sea. The boat is floating upside down on the heavens above in the eternal seas. In the upside down world of this church boat, the last will be first, the poor will be rich, the humble will be exalted, and those who lose their life will find it.

In Dante's "Inferno," over the archway to hell there is an inscription: "Abandon hope all you who enter here." Over the threshold to heaven that is God's church, we have a different welcome: "Have hope in Jesus all ye who enter here." The church itself is shaped as an encompassing cross. Surely the cross remains our only hope. *Spes Unica.* Because

God has loved us, because we receive the self-gift of the Father's only Son in the incarnation of Jesus, because Jesus died for love of us, we have reason to hope. Because God is resourceful and even our own freedom cannot escape God's provident love, we have reason to hope. Every time we pass through the doorway of this Basilica, and indeed of all Christian churches, we are invited to pass from despair to hope. "Come, you that are blessed by my Father, inherit the kingdom prepared for you from the foundation of the world" (Mt 25:34). The church building by itself does not make the reality in which we hope. The stone and glass structure is but a reminder, a place of refuge and of retreat, a foretaste of joy and a pledge of our destiny to be with God forever in friendship and intimacy. The walk through the doorway into the Basilica is a rehearsal for the real thing, our passage from death to life, our coming from the outside of God to the inside, our walking from this passing life into eternal life, "what no eye has seen, nor ear heard, nor the human heart conceived, what God has prepared for those who love him" (1 Cor 2:9).

The Splendor of the Basilica

WHENEVER I ENTER the Basilica, I always kneel in a place where I can see clearly the statue of our Lady at the far end of the nave, in a niche on the back wall of the Lady Chapel. It brings me comfort and I feel enfolded in her presence. That statue of Mary is regal and feminine. Here is the crowned queen of heaven. The artist sculpted a beautiful and mature woman holding her child with confidence in her heart.

Critics of devotion to Mary point out that the artistic depictions of her rarely show an actual real woman. She is set on a pedestal, and who can imitate such virtues? Even the way she holds the child, nonchalantly off her hip with one hand, is impossible for a real woman. And yet, I think, who cares about the law of gravity when one is looking at the loving and lovely ineffable mystery of God's infinite being in a baby who made a woman cry?

The ceiling of the Basilica is strewn with stars and with innumerable angels. Some angels are young women and some are babies. In the scriptures angels were young men. Gabriel appears to Mary to announce the enfleshment of God, should she consent. The two young men at the tomb of Jesus are angels, who announce to the women that he is risen, "he is not here." Over the years angels were depicted as young women, and then as baby cherubs. In our patriarchal world the depiction of angels may have declined in our imagination. In the Basilica the angels are unisex. They could be young men, I suppose, though their flowing hair, their arms, and their well-draped hips are those of a woman. There is no curve to the female breast, and no bare bottom anywhere among the naked baby cherubs. The angels are very modest. Perhaps there is a tinge of the Jansenism of France, which was uncomfortable with the human body even while fervent in matters of the soul. I am distracted by the angel modesty more than I would be if I could see the outline of a woman's breast and the shape of a baby's bottom. I feel like the city dweller trying to sleep in the countryside, where the very silence has become the distraction. Of course, no one wants the church to be a sensual spectacle, or an invitation for less than pure thoughts for men or for women. And yet, there must be a balance between no acknowledgment of the difference between a man's body and a woman's, and temptation.

In an attempt to show that Jesus, though he was born and died a man, claims humanity more than gender as the pledge of our salvation, an artist sculpted a female corpus on the cross of Calvary.[2] *Christa* is a powerful representation of the mystery of the incarnation that transcends gender and claims the essential meaning of the incarnation. And yet I could not look on a cross with a seminude woman with complete equanimity. There must be a balance between no sensuality in the church and inappropriate bodiliness.

One of the insights I gained in a long stay in Italy was the Italian regard for poverty in a person of faith. Francis

2. The Christa crucifix has been displayed in the Cathedral of Saint John the Divine in New York City.

of Assisi fell in love with "Lady Poverty." His sensibility pervades the Italian soul. That men and women have a body does not surprise Italians, nor that their bodies are different and delightful. After all, they would say, one is human. It is riches which deprive the poor that are held to be the sin to lament in the Church. Accumulation of wealth by a church claiming to serve the poor becomes a scandal. Were the elaborate tabernacle in the Basilica at Notre Dame depicting the heavenly Jerusalem coming down from heaven made of solid gold instead of wood painted gold and embossed with semiprecious stones, that extravagance would be a scandal. Churches should be beautiful, but there should be a balance with riches as well as with sensuality. Luxury and ostentation also corrupt hearts. Chalices should not be so golden that their wealth is beyond measure. And yet, like the woman who poured the precious perfume on the feet of Jesus, we need to waste some riches on the one we love. Judas thought the expensive ointment should have been sold and the money given to the poor. And, one could argue, were all the husbands and wives of the world to sell their wedding rings we would have a fortune with which to feed the hungry of this world. Nonetheless, we know that a simple gold ring must be given and worn on the hand night and day, for the beloved remains ever priceless. Our churches in their modest splendor become our golden rings given to our beloved, who has married us as the spouse of God's delight. Moreover, we are the daughters and sons within the body of Christ Jesus, in whom the Father is well pleased. As the prodigal father explains to the elder son in the gospel parable: "But we had to celebrate and rejoice, because this brother of yours was dead and has come to life; he was lost and has been found" (Lk 15:32).

Christian Death

THE PATRON OF a Christian death is Saint Joseph. In the Basilica of the Sacred Heart, there are three pictorial representations of the death of Saint Joseph. Why Joseph is patron of a Christian death, which is indeed a happy death, emerges from a perusal of these depictions. On the east wall of the entrance to the Lady Chapel at the rear of the church is a large fresco of Joseph lying on his death bed, with Jesus on one side and Mary on the other. Two stained glass windows also depict the death of Joseph. One is found in the west windows as you enter the sanctuary, and the other in a small bay-chapel window on the east side opposite the tabernacle.

Because Joseph does not appear again in the Gospels after the finding of the child Jesus in the Temple, the tradition arose that Joseph died well before Jesus died. Perhaps Joseph was older than Mary, perhaps a widower who brought into the marriage with Mary sons and daughters, half-brothers and half-sisters to Jesus. That would explain the brothers and sisters of Jesus mentioned in the gospel accounts and support the perpetual virginity of Mary, as the Christian tradition has long cherished. The older age of Joseph would also explain his early death. The circumstances of his last days make him the model of a happy death and the patron of a Christian death. Who would not want to die like Joseph, with Mary praying on one side of one's bed and Jesus on the other? It is our Christian hope that we also will die with Mary and Jesus (and Joseph) at our side in faith and in hope of God's everlasting mercy.

In the Basilica's huge stained glass windows in the eastern transept and western transept, we see the sweep of life from birth to death through the eyes of Mary. In the east window where the morning sun shines she sits among the disciples at the coming of the Holy Spirit in tongues of fire at the first Pentecost. Here is the birth of the Church. Here is our own baptism when we were given the Holy Spirit as our pledge of eternal life. Here is our beginning in the life that will not end. Here is the rising of the sun in the east of our existence. Then across the ceiling of the Basilica the sun travels out of sight but in a sure passage of time through the figures of the prophets and evangelists depicted on the very center ceiling where the arms of the cross that shape the architecture of the Basilica building itself crisscross. Holy Scripture enlightens the way to God through the dark days of our lifetime. And in the end, at our dying, as the sun goes down for us in the west transept window, the figure of Mary lies in the fading light on her death bed, surrounded by the disciples, who are the Church. And so we also hope to die in the Church with Mary and Jesus and Joseph and the communion of saints all around us. From Pentecost to the Dormition of Mary, from the east to the west, from our birth to our death, we move in time within the mystery of the Church which remains ever the mystery of the cross—the love of God given for us in the birth and death of Jesus Christ.

Fifty years ago when I was a seminarian living in the old Moreau Seminary (later Saint Joseph Hall and today Sacred Heart Parish Center), the seminarians were introduced to the mystery of human death in ways that have now been lost, and perhaps sadly lost. When a Holy Cross community member died, we used to be assigned the "wake" during the late hours until morning to watch with the body laid out in Corby Hall Chapel. In the middle of the night we walked around the lake to Corby Hall in often total darkness. There were no path lights and the woods along the lake shore were dense on a moonless night. If one's replacement did not arrive because he overslept, one might be two hours in the chapel alone with the dead in the middle of the night. It did give substance to one's meditation.

At the funeral itself, when the religious community would assemble to follow the coffin from the church to Holy Cross cemetery, which is but a short walk on Saint Mary's Road, we would line up by house age (determined by the day one joined the Holy Cross Congregation). The oldest member followed immediately behind the coffin, and the youngest seminarian brought up the rear. In three years in the seminary at Notre Dame, I found myself move from the end of the line closer to the middle. We walked in silence. It was a walk to ponder, and that memory reminds me to this day that my time will also come.

The Steeple Bells

HIGH UP ON the Basilica steeple the large moon-shaped face of a clock shines in the dark on all four sides. From quite a distance the time is visible, especially at night, but throughout the day as well. Every quarter hour the church bells mark the time and ring appropriately on the hour. The bells are turned off in the late evening, and the last sounds are the carillon bells playing "Notre Dame Our Mother," the *alma mater* song of the university.

Church steeples and plinth-like monuments are seen at times as phallic symbols, signs of pride and male domination. I see the Basilica steeple as an aspiration beyond gender to look to the stars and point to eternity. It seems right that human clock time be inserted in the steeple time that suggests the eternity of God where the past, present, and future are but an everlasting now within which God dwells—just as our created being has its integrity in the great mystery of God's creation of the world from nothing, and yet we are not outside the infinite being of God as if we were ever on our own. Our created time has its integrity in the great mystery of God's creation of time, and yet our days are never outside the eternal awareness of God for whom the past and the future are always now. Our time, as our very being, is implicated in the mystery of God. I look to the steeple and my heart leaps with hope that I too may know God's eternity. I see the clock by day and by night, and I know time and eternity will some day coincide. I hear the bells announce the hour, and I know I am closer to eternity and "nearer my God to thee" with every passing moment. When the bells peal in exuberance and celebration, calling the campus to community prayer or announcing that the church assembly has prayed with joy and goes forth with hearts singing, I hear something of the choirs of heaven. When the largest single bell is tolled slowly for funerals, I know I am not to ask for whom the bell tolls. It tolls for me, and for thee.

Vertical is the steeple and vertical is the piety of the Basilica of the Sacred Heart at Notre Dame. Worship is a primary thrust of the whole architecture. The horizontal sense of a community gathered around a table of communion in a world of creation with its own integrity and its own ordinary grace is less obvious. Across the way at the Church of Loreto on the campus of Saint Mary's College, one finds a recent renovation of their once equally vertical church architecture. The sisters of the Holy Cross chose to emphasize the circularity of their prayer space and the horizontal dimension of their community assembly. There is a sense in that church that ordinary time and ordinary life is familial. Just being shoulder to shoulder in the round and on the level is a sign of inclusion and the recognition of God's love enfolding ordinary human beings. Their circle is more female, the liturgy more friendly, I believe, to women in these days when women are not always comfortable in a church where their role has hardly been equal. In the round and on the level, with plain glass windows replacing stained glass, the Church of Loreto is a contrast with the Notre Dame Basilica. I like to think of the former as home cooking and the latter as an elegant restaurant. Both serve the nourishing food of God's Eucharist to a family gathered around a table, but the one sees the horizontal and needs no steeple to remind it of eternity, and the other lifts high the cross and sees in its high reaches the majesty of God that draws the ordinary up into everlasting glory.

Weddings and Baptisms

THE ELDERS AMONG us on this campus are fond of saying that the students keep getting younger each year. We know it is we who are becoming older, and it but seems that younger life keeps appearing among us. Notre Dame is not just a family; the university seems to be raising a family. The Basilica is booked for weddings from here to eternity, and every Saturday that is not taken with home football or some other compelling campus event is taken with wedding after wedding in an hourly procession. I see the bride and groom afterwards in the Grotto where pictures are so often taken for posterity. Smaller weddings and anniversary celebrations take place in the Log Chapel, where many a poorer couple began their marriage when travel money was not so ample. Notre Dame draws from all fifty states in proportionate ways, and when the bride is from California and the groom from New Jersey, the wedding at Notre Dame is an extravaganza. Outside the Basilica one sees everything from stretch limos to horse and carriage, and the creativity of dress in the wedding party belongs in a golden Basilica.

Not only marriages keep Notre Dame young, but baptisms in the Basilica on Sunday afternoons and in the Log Chapel at all times of the day bring birth into eternal life. One might suppose that birthing is what human life is all about. We celebrate our birthday into this world from our mother's womb, and the Church celebrates our death day at our birth day into eternal life from our mother Earth. Holy mother the Church knows that our real conception as a child of God took place in the mystery of our Baptism and the gift of the Holy Spirit in our soul, and that our real birth is from the darkness of this world into the everlasting light of heaven, where we shall see the face of God who has loved us from all eternity.

All life is birth. Marriage is the birth of two becoming one flesh, the birth of a new family. We celebrate the birthdays of our children. Creation itself was birthed from the hand of the Creator in the beginning and awaits its birth as the new heaven and the new earth in the second coming of Jesus Christ, when creation will become the Kingdom of God. We celebrate Christmas as the birthday of Jesus on Earth and Easter resurrection as his entrance into heaven, where he sits forever at the right hand of the Father Almighty.

Notre Dame graduates its students into the life of an educated person. The university is an *alma mater* (a nourishing mother). Birthing (or graduation) is what our *alma mater* is about. Birthing (or baptism) is what holy mother Church is about. Birthing (or creation) is what the "father almighty, creator of heaven and earth" is about. At Notre Dame we are professors. We hope to speak out (to profess) on behalf of the truth. At Notre Dame we are all being called to be procreators, to give life, to birth intellectual and spiritual life on behalf of the Creator. There are many ways to give life. Not only is the body birthed into this world, but our minds, our hearts, and our souls must be brought out of darkness into the light, and the young life that God so loves must be nourished with the truth, the love, and the hope of God.

Calvary Hill

TUCKED AROUND THE southwest edges of Saint Joseph's Lake, an outdoor stations of the cross winds along the shore then turns into the only remaining woods at Notre Dame and climbs a hillock to the top of Calvary Hill. There on a life-size standing crucifix hangs Jesus in his dying, with a statue of his mother Mary in sorrow on one side and the beloved disciple John on the other. "'Woman here is your son.' Then he said to the disciple. 'Here is your mother'" (Jn 17:27).

In a recent conversation with parents of small children, the conversation turned to children crying in the night. Does a loving parent always answer the cry of their child? Some parents believe their child needs to learn that in this life not every cry is answered. Life is not fair. Life can be hard and one needs to learn to depend on oneself. Other parents believe that hope is engendered in a child for a lifetime provided they know someone will come when they cry out for help. Someone is there for them. I have met adults who feel in their life's troubles when they cry, no one will come. The psalms in the Bible are song-prayers of humanity crying to God. "Hear us, O Lord! Come to us, O Lord! Save us, O Lord! Help us, O Lord!" And on Calvary hill Jesus cried out and no one appeared to give him solace. "My God, my God, why have you forsaken me?" (Mk 15:34) Of course, there is more to Psalm 22 that Jesus here recites in part by memory, and we believe Jesus said in his heart the whole psalm, which concludes with these hopeful lines: "future generations will be told about the Lord, and proclaim his deliverance to a people yet unborn, saying that he has done it." On Easter Sunday, Jesus knew he had not been forsaken by his Father.

A friend of mine tells this story of her encounter with Jesus on Calvary Hill. Her life was saddened by her love bestowed on others who would not receive her love. She knew she wanted only to give love, but there was no welcome. With a heavy heart on a winter day she climbed our Notre Dame hill to Calvary. Her heart was heavy with sorrow and she looked up at the man of sorrows hanging in front of her on that life-like iron cross. He looked at her and she looked at him. Heart spoke to heart. Love embraced love. And then the remnants of a winter snowfall on the crown of thorns melted in the sun, and tears began to run down the cheek of Jesus on the cross. It was as if Jesus wanted to say to her: I know what it is to love and be rejected. All my life I wanted, like you, only to love the people all around me, but they would not. Then she saw the people around her with the heart of Jesus: Look, I am giving you myself. See me! I am giving you me. I want you to know my desire. Indeed, we do know and alas we do forget that all Jesus ever wanted was to love and to be loved. The exchange of love is love's very essence. In this brief experience this woman knew Jesus knew her pain as his very own.

I have sat at the Grotto of Notre Dame in the late evening or in the early morning and I have noticed lone women from time to time coming to pray. There is grief in their faces, sadness in their eyes, and sometimes tears on their cheeks. I think I know what happened. They have been unhappy with their boyfriend in the night. Perhaps they quarreled. Perhaps they broke up. Perhaps they were intimate, and she blames herself for a foolish decision or blames him for abusing her when her wishes were not respected. Deep is the searing pain of an unrequited love. Pressing is the overall question. Who wants me? Who wants to love me? Who wants really to be with me tenderly and always? Is there anybody there? "My God, my God, why have you abandoned me" may seem too dramatic for this scene, but I am never sure we comprehend how close to despair the human heart sails, and how quick when it grinds against the reef it does sink.

At the foot of the cross on Calvary Hill we do know the heart of Jesus. It is a heart broken for love of us, and when we are heartbroken we are never more inside the heart of Jesus, who bled love for us as surely as he bled his blood for us. "Let me love or let me die," said Teresa of Avila. Love is a dying, a pouring out of one's very heart for the beloved, freely and unconditionally, in hope of love returned. That human desire will neither be contained nor postponed. God is love, and because we are created in the image of God, so are we made in love's image.

God's Acre

THERE ARE TWO cemeteries at the university of Notre Dame. The older cemetery, Cedar Grove, is at the head of Notre Dame Avenue as it comes into the campus. It holds the remains of the nineteenth-century pioneers to South Bend and many to this university and its endeavors. I like to walk the paths of this sacred land, God's acre, especially in the autumn when the very old maple trees that line the walkways are sifting down soft gold in the late afternoon sun. You would think it would be sad to linger and pray the rosary in a graveyard. But the resurrection of the body is not a sad hope. One's own mortality comes to mind, of course, but there is no loneliness when considering one's place among the communion of saints in the eternity of God, who made us all and loves us every day of our lives no matter how short, no matter how long. I read the gravestones and try to imagine what their lives might have encompassed. Many reflect the deaths of young children, and in the days before inoculations, childhood diseases must have been epidemic. The war years took their toll. Sometimes a spouse dies young, and one wonders how their mate managed alone for decades to come. In other marriages both spouses died at about the same time, and one wonders if a broken heart can be fatal.

Two gravesites remain in my memory, and my visit to them is always poignant. There lies Margaret Beeler, a young woman student and member of the Notre Dame swim team who died on a winter night in the roll-over of a chartered bus that skidded on ice just before arriving back to the safety of the campus. Her family found a plot for her eternal rest where she could see the golden Dome, and their grief was our grief. And there was Catherine LaCugna, a woman in her prime and a distinguished professor of theology, who wrote eloquently and devoutly of the Trinity. She was composing her thoughts about the Holy Spirit in the Church and in the soul of the graced when she died after a lingering and painful struggle with a remorseless cancer of the breast. We walked from the Basilica following her body as it was taken to the grave not far from the campus where she taught and where she prayed. Edgar Allan Poe thought the saddest tale for a poet was the death of a beautiful woman, but I think the death of a beautiful mind and soul can break your heart just as well—and she was lovely to boot.

The other cemetery at Notre Dame belongs to the Congregation of Holy Cross and is found midway on the road from the Grotto to Saint Mary's College. Just as in Cedar Grove, the tombstone dates tell the story of plague and pestilence that descended at intervals upon the fragile and small Holy Cross community in the early days of Notre Dame du Lac. Many are the men in this graveyard who gave their life and their lifetime for the welfare of the University of Notre Dame. They lie row upon row with identical grave markers in the form of a limestone cross: name and date of birth into this world and date of death, which each one believed to be their day of birth into eternal life.

Perhaps the best friend I have known in the Congregation of Holy Cross lies buried here under the shade of a pine tree. I remember him in the days we served together in the novitiate of the Holy Cross Congregation in Cascade, Colorado. He would leave the house at midnight and climb in the light of the full moon 7000 vertical feet to the top of Pike's Peak and return back in time for breakfast. No one could keep up with him. He used to say that God was a treasure hunter and not a garbage collector and we should trust in God's unbounded love and mercy. He died with his boots on, as he would have wanted to, in a spectacular fall from the top of Mount Blanco in a climb that somehow belonged to the darkness. Those of us in Holy Cross yet living wonder where in this God's acre our own little piece of planet Earth will be. I should have liked to be near Jim, but I would settle for a spot under a pine tree not too far apart.

Of all the experiences of death that I can speak of in my years with Holy Cross, I would tell the story of the death of Father Charles Miltner, C.S.C. He had been for many years the president of the University of Portland, a Holy Cross school in Oregon where I was serving at the time. Well up in years, he was to move his residence to Holy Cross House, the retirement home of the Congregation on the campus of Notre Dame. He was to leave the day after the banquet, to which dignitaries and friends within the Portland university community and in the city had been invited. The evening was gala, and the attendance was large and distinguished. At the end of the meal Father Miltner stood up and said a few words of greeting to the guests. He made some humorous remarks about recipes for living to a ripe old age. One took a spoonful of honey and a spoonful of vinegar each day. And so forth. Then he became quite serious and said: "But the truth is that one lives exactly as long as God wishes." Father Miltner sat down at his place at the table and died.

Along the Way Places

Weather

ROTC

Sunrise and Sunset

Pools and Lakes

The Silent Presence

Water, Water Everywhere

Notre Dame Ballet

Reflecting Pool

Trees

The Peace Fountain

Museum Courtyard

Weather

THE STORY IS told that when Father Sorin and the band of Holy Cross brothers arrived at the land the Bishop of Vincennes had given for a school in northern Indiana, the weather was miserable. The brothers suggested that they might look for a donation of land further south (Florida would have pleased me), and Father Sorin agreed. Since the weather was bad he promised they would move south just as soon as it improved. And Notre Dame has been in South Bend ever since. Despite our complaints, the four seasons seem to me what is best about weather at Notre Dame. Just when one is tired of winter cold comes yellow-green spring. Just when one is weary of summer heat comes golden-red autumn. I like to think I would not take the opportunity to move to California with sunshine and moderate temperatures day after day. I do like the quiet and purity of an evening snowfall. I do glory in the riot of color in the fall leaves falling. I do take on a bright hue when the daffodils poke their noses up through the remnants of the snow bank and blossom in such a sunny yellow. And I do delight in a summer night to hear the crickets and buggy critters all abuzz. I would miss the four seasons of Notre Dame. Every time of year and every day has its character and holds its value.

Lake Michigan has an effect on the weather of the university campus. Scarcely thirty miles away as the crow flies, the lake is a huge body of warm water in winter and cool water in summer. That differential makes for lake-effect clouds, which gray the campus skies all too often in winter and provide moisture for fine-grained snowfall when the wind is off the lake and the temperature cold but not too cold. In the summer I have a theory that the lake steers the tornadoes that come across Indiana to swing somewhat east and north of Notre Dame through the center of the lower peninsula of Michigan. Perhaps we have been spared a devastating storm by the lake waters that temper the climate of those lands along its southeastern shores—or by chance, or rather by God's providence.

A walk through the central campus where the oldest trees are found reveals not a one without many wounds. Limbs are gone from ice, snow, or windstorm. Drought, fungus, and beetles have all taken a toll in the lives of our trees and in the maiming of them. The many flowering trees are vulnerable to the ravages of a late frost. Not a tree on campus that is not scarred or distorted in some way, and yet I love each one of those trees and cry a bit inside every time one of them is taken down for whatever reason. Each tree is a treasure, even in its imperfection, and the campus is less rich every time we are less one tree, however strange. Our acceptance of our landscape is unconditional, because it is ours.

I find every tree on this campus contributes to my happiness, and though I see the woundedness and imperfection in them all, still they are beautiful. Each tree is unique just as each student on this campus and each person at this university and in this world is an especially loved child of God. The glory of God is in you. There will never be another you. Each one of us is one-of-a-kind. Each one of us is incomparable. Were we to see the indwelling of the Holy Spirit in the people around us we would, like Moses, see the flames of God in the burning bush. Moses was given to see what was already there, the glory of God for anyone whose eyes are attentive and whose heart is on fire. When he was university president I often heard Father Hesburgh say that the Notre Dame students are the best students in the world. And they are. I know not where there could be better students, who come in the main from homes where faith in God and love of family intermingle, and whose good will and innocence is unexplainable without the abundance of grace. That is not to say that Notre Dame students always behave well. They are human, and they are sinful too. But they are the best students in the world, in part because they are on this campus best loved. The poet John Donne knew that nothing or no one that God brings about is badly brought about. "He can bring thy summer out of winter,/ Though thou have no spring. . . . All occasions invite his mercies/And all times are His seasons."

ROTC

NOTRE DAME SERVES the military of the United States through a large and well-established Reserved Officer Training Corps (ROTC). During World War II the Navy took over much of the campus facilities for officer training. I myself learned how to march in the Navy Drill Hall when I was an undergraduate Navy recruit during the Korean War. Over the years a good relationship with the U.S. Navy has been enjoyed by Notre Dame, and the other armed forces found a home here as well. Hundreds of Notre Dame students are enabled to attend Notre Dame because of military scholarships in return for service after graduation. Critics of warfare argue that the military has no place in a Catholic institution committed to peace. Advocates of a just-war ethic argue that, difficult as it may be to limit wars and to discern just wars, we have not found a way to eliminate violent conflict. Given the reality that the military will be with us in the foreseeable future, do we not want men and women of integrity in its ranks? If good people will not serve, who does that leave? I dream of a day when there will no longer be national armies, which have a penchant to serve particular interests at the expense of the common good of spaceship Earth. I dream of the day that the United Nations will become secure and mature enough to maintain a stable international police force, which will be to the world and its problems of violence and injustice what the city police force or campus security is to our welfare at Notre Dame.

When school begins in the autumn, I watch the ROTC cadets jogging around the lakes in the early morning as I sit in contemplation of the turning leaves with a cup of coffee in my hand and a prayer in my heart. They jog in whatever sports clothes they brought from home. Soon they are all wearing identical T-shirts that announce they are Navy or Army or Air Force. Then they are jogging in unison and singing the chants that the mobile military love as churchgoers do their hymns. Not long after, I see them jogging in camouflage fatigues, and then with backpacks added. Then one morning one rubs one's eyes in disbelief. Marching in unison with chants shouted out loud and rifles at the ready appears a platoon of young soldiers. It no longer seems like college-campus practice. I think of the phrase in the creed "suffered under Pontius Pilate." Both Israel and Jesus Christ were at the mercy of armed might, and the world has not much changed. In the end, we all suffer "under Pontius Pilate," both when we are enslaved and when we are free. And free is better; I do not doubt that. But we suffer the effects of violence whether on the offense or on the defense. It is, alas, even now the "way of the world." We may find it easy to despise the military, as it remains easy to make lawyer jokes; but when one needs rescue or deliverance from injustice, one becomes suddenly grateful for those who stand against iniquity. Of course, we know "power corrupts and absolute power corrupts absolutely" (Lord Acton). And yet God bless both those who in conscience cannot resist evil with violence and those willing to lay down their lives so that others might live.

Jesus tells the parable of the Good Samaritan who stops and binds up the wounds of the man fallen among robbers as he was going down to Jericho. Jesus praises the Samaritan who takes the wounded man to an inn and offers to pay whatever it takes for his ongoing care. We easily come to understand what we must do when the mugging is over and the war has come to an end. We must bind up the wounded and rebuild what is left of their lives. I often have wished Jesus had told a parable of what we are to do if we come along the road to Jericho when the mugging is going on under our eyes. Do we call out? Do we watch in horror? Do we run for help? Do we risk our own safety and intervene physically in hopes of stopping the violence? Do we calculate how we might prevail in a physical encounter with the assailant, whether by our own strength or by a weapon? Perhaps Jesus as a man, with only the human understanding of a man of his time and place, did not know himself.

I believe in nonviolent resistance to evil, and I believe it could overcome injustice and protect the world if most everyone adopted that ethic. If only a few people choose nonviolence, the violent will bear the world away. And yet the example of the nonviolent may save the world. And doing what our conscience demands is all God asks any of us. We are not finally responsible for the behavior of others and for the outcome of the history of the world. Whatever our strategy, we all will die sooner or later. And to die carrying the cross does seem more Christ-like than to die carrying the sword. I cannot imagine Jesus killing anyone for any reason. Nor can I imagine I would idle by while children are being harmed. Lord, have mercy on us. We ask a lot of our young men and women on this campus and in the world. Lord, have mercy on us.

Sunrise and Sunset

INDIANA HAS NO mountains and our landscape is far from any ocean, even though the shores of Lake Michigan on a stormy day might yield a reasonable facsimile of the sea. Indiana does boast sunrises and sunsets, and they can be spectacular. The local folks speculate that it is the dust rising from the vast farmlands of Indiana that refract the light of dawn and dusk in such a way as to create a kaleidoscope of pastel colors. Perhaps the low horizon of big-sky country gives Hoosiers a better view of the morning and the evening skies. Whatever the reasons, rainbowed grandeur in the heavens is there for anyone to see. And as the song reminds us, "the best things in life are free." However, you do have to look up or look out. I am peeved when someone raves about today's sunrise or sunset, and I remember that I was seated by a window and only needed to take time to turn my head and appreciate what was given me.

In the summer, sunrise is very early, and I find that it is only from mid autumn and into the spring that I am awake and outside in time for the coming of the morning glory. Not every sunrise displays beautiful color, but every morning presents a picture that is beautiful. Black-and-white photography can be expressive of nuance that color misses. I never cease to marvel at the infinite shades of gray and the varied patterns of light and subtle color that each and every sunrise offers us. The day is born gradually but inevitably, and no one knows for sure in advance who this child will be. I like to think that watching the sunrise is a companion to our morning prayer. We need to be reminded that we have come again into existence from the death of sleep. We need to be aware that we are being born anew with every new day. We come from the darkness of nonexistence, and our very being is the reflection of the light of God upon us created by God's creative care for us from the beginning. Every day we should be reminded of our birthday, of God's abiding love for us, and what better cake for our soul to feast upon than the joy that comes in the quiet of the morning as the sky fills with color or contrast, with clearness or cloud configurations, and we are lost in wonder that anything exists at all? Why me, Lord, in all this vast and ever re-created cosmos?

Sunsets at Notre Dame are seen across the surface of Saint Mary's Lake. Day seems to be ending in peace and in quiet glory. Fire colors shimmer on the glassy lake surface that mirrors the heavens. The ducks, the geese, and the swans are tranquil in the waning light. They say that swans really do sing a beautiful song when they are dying, and that death as one's swan song ought to be pondered. I once heard baby storks in the nest, and for all the world they sounded like a human baby crying for its mother. The stork stories also were based on the observation of people who saw the world around and above them and listened to its cries. I am not sure that sunsets are any less spectacular than sunrises, but I think my capacity for enjoyment is greater in the morning. One has freshly arisen from the night and its oblivion. One's mind is undistracted and the first sense impressions that come into the eye for contemplation are from the painted skies of water colors that blend into a majesty that makes you want to hold perfectly still forever in hopes that nothing above you and around you will ever change. Sunsets are a gentle reminder that our work is done, that the leaves will fall, that the light will fade, and that our lives will end in the darkness of the night.

The evening star which often hangs in the sky at sunset is also that same planet Venus, which is the morning star when we rise from our sleep to live another day on planet Earth. In the divine eternal day we shall look upon the light itself in the glory of the beatific vision of God as God. No more shall sunrise remind us of our birth in the love of God and sunset remind us of our death in the love of Jesus Christ. Then we shall see the light of God in all its splendor, of which the refractions in the prism of our skies will seem but a preview in the dark.

If one remembers morning prayer, it is more likely one will remember there may be a sunrise to experience this morning. Thereby we remember each morning how wonderful that we were birthed into this our human daylight. If one remembers evening prayer, it is more likely one will remember there may be a sunset to experience this evening. Thereby we remember each evening how wonderful that we are birthed into God's eternal life.

Pools and Lakes

NOTRE DAME IS blessed by God with two lakes and by generous benefactors with two swimming pools. I walk around the lakes and swim around the pools. I feel privileged. If we feel peace in and around water, it may be because we emerged from the sea in prehistory. Our body is mostly water, and we were floated in our mother's womb for months as a blissful creature in a salt sea. It is hard to imagine Notre Dame without the waters of Saint Mary's Lake and Saint Joseph's Lake. Notre Dame would not be Our Lady of the Lake (Notre Dame du Lac) without the springs that daily rise cool and clear at the east end of Saint Joseph's Lake and give to us living water that flows through the campus heartland into Saint Mary's Lake and eventually west into the Saint Joseph River and thence into the Atlantic Ocean. We are part of a big sea of God's providence, and Notre Dame graduates meander through all parts of an arid land to bring, one hopes, waters flowing from the springs of living water that Jesus promised to the woman at the well and to all who desire his gift: "If you knew the gift of God, and who it is that is saying to you, 'Give me a drink,' you would have asked him, and he would have given you living water" (Jn 4:10).

When I swim at Notre Dame, I see mermaids all around me. Within the clear, clean water and with goggles on my eyes the mermaids emerge from the foam and swim by my side—

but briefly, for buoyantly in the water they glide by swiftly compared to this old walrus. My eyes dance and my heart is joyful. My soul is also a tad sad, because I rarely see any young woman in the pool except one who looks beautiful (in a man's eyes, I suppose I must add) in a bathing suit. The young women who wrongly think they are not worthy in swimwear do not come to swim. They do without. I hope they never really believe I think any the less of them as women no matter their appearance. We all have our place, and no one else can take our place. I miss them.

When walking around the lake I notice the men and women who are jogging. Women more often than not jog in pairs and in the daylight. The solitary runner is likely to be a man; the runner alone at night is surely a man. I know why, and it also makes me sad. Sometimes when I walk across the campus at night, all two hundred pounds of me with a heavy beard on my cheeks and a dark wool skull cap pulled over my ears to keep the winter winds at bay, I pass a young woman on the pathways. I see fear in her eyes and uncertainty in her steps as we come close, lonely ships in the night. I would say "good evening," but I am afraid to startle her or appear to be starting something. My heart is sorrowful, for I would not harm such a lovely creature for all the world.

The Silent Presence

THE NOTRE DAME campus is a sylvan oasis with an urban world surrounding it. The grounds are beautifully landscaped with a variety of trees, shrubs, and flowering plants from springtime to autumn when the colored leaves fall and the curtain of winter starts to fall. Even then the evergreens enliven the campus. Notre Dame is also a city where ten thousand people crisscross in the daytime. Students and employees move busily about their workday. More automobiles than one can count overflow the many parking areas, and traffic on campus roads is steady. Sidewalks are crowded with pedestrians, with noisy golf carts carrying injured varsity athletes and pizza deliveries. Trucks of every description roam from building to building. There is a truck for Coca-Cola, a truck for Pepsi-Cola, a truck for Frito-Lay, a truck for milk deliveries, a truck for mail, a truck for every delivery and every building. "The world is too much with us," as Wordsworth lamented. When wet or dry the grass is cut, the massive power mowers are loud, and they are followed by gasoline-powered grass collectors, then weed-wackers that edge the lawns, and finally blowers that whine with jet-engine pitch while sweeping the sidewalks of debris. Silence is hard to come by. There are chain saws to bring down the diseased trees and construction machinery at the many sites where buildings are being continually repaired. Notre Dame is a city where the work of landscapers, carpenters, builders, teamsters, and artisans of every kind ply their trade. Silence is hard to come by.

Libraries used to be a place of silence, but people talk in libraries now. They have become a social space as well as a study space. Librarians talk in libraries, and there is much to talk about. The Basilica used to be a place of silence, but now there are tourists who express their appreciation and guides who serve them with conversation. Silence is hard to come by.

We need silence as human beings. Silence is not empty. Silence is not the absence of sound. Silence is the fullness of God. Silence is a *plenum* from whose vast and lavish richness we make sounds that express but a particle of the whole mystery. "Speech, after long silence; it is right" was the poet's plea.[3] In seminar with students I yearn for moments of silence before someone begins to answer a question posed them. We need to think in silence as well as to think out loud. Of course, some folks find interior silence more readily than others. Yet I think we all need more silence. In the liturgy there is to be a moment of silence for all of us to gather in our hearts our own prayer before the oration is prayed in the name of the community. We cannot endure, however, more than a few seconds of this silence. In our after-communion silence, if we enjoy a pause at all, the passage of a minute of silence may seem very long. We are not used to silence, and it makes us uncomfortable. But something valuable has been lost when silence has been lost. Noise always dominates silence. You cannot impose silence on anyone, but you can impose noise. Silence was there in the beginning, and it is we who break the silence all too often. What I wish is that I

3. "After Long Silence," by William Butler Yeats

could watch the rain come down in the springtime in silence. I would like time without noise to watch the grass grow. What I wish is that I could watch the leaves flutter in autumn stillness and snow fall in winter in quiet wonder.

Observers of the younger generation have lamented that they no longer seem to recognize the "real presence" in the Eucharist. I suspect they may not have heard of the term "real presence," and so may seem to be oblivious of the mystery of the body and blood of Jesus really present in the Eucharist. But I think they know in some other ways that the Eucharist is sacred. We have not so much lost the real presence of God as we have lost the silent presence of God. It is the awesomeness of the dwelling of God in the Eucharist bread and in the tabernacle that seems lost. The vast silence of the sacred presence and the sacred place seems to have been lost, even as we have gained a closeness with God and a familiarity with one another in community prayer. I look at the tabernacle in the Basilica at Notre Dame with awe. It is an artistic replica of the description of the new Jerusalem coming down from heaven as described in the Book of Revelation: "Come I will show you the bride, the wife of the Lamb. And in the spirit he carried me away to a great, high mountain and showed me the holy city Jerusalem coming down out of heaven from God. It has the glory of God and a radiance like a very rare jewel, like jasper, clear as crystal. It has a great high wall with twelve gates, and at the gates twelve angels, and on the gates are inscribed the names of the twelve tribes of the Israelites" (21:9–12). What I wish is that we could kneel in front of that mystery of gentle grace from on high from time to time in awe and in silence.

Water, Water Everywhere

AS I AM writing this reflection, northern Indiana is suffering a severe drought that has lasted throughout the summer, with limited relief. Crops have been ruined wherever there was no irrigation, and untended lawns are brown and dry. The paths around the lakes are dusty. The lawns at Notre Dame, however, are emerald green, and the reason is that the sprinkling system comes on day and night in this, then that, section of lawn to keep the grass growing. It seems a luxury and sometimes a separation from the suffering of those less fortunate. It seems extravagant to water lawns when water is not in endless supply and heaven seems to have closed its sluice gates. Maybe it will never rain again. I miss a certain solidarity with the cruel world, the world of the majority of people and the bulk of the land.

So much in our world seems done because it can be done. We are now approaching the marvel and the foolhardiness of cloning a human being. Much more we will do because we can do, not because we know it is best to do. Are we inebriated with our powers over matter? I think of these innocent green lawns in a time of drought on our campus, and I wonder if we are extravagant with electric power to pump the water from the bowels of the earth where tomorrow's inheritance yet lies pure and undisturbed. I wonder if we are imprudent to water so recklessly, automatically, no one watching, with sprays of water over roads and sidewalks indiscriminately, and broken valves gushing pools of water and no repair in sight. Some one must be watching, but I see waste day after day, night after night.

The sprinklers used to provide endless fun on the paths and sidewalks of the campus. And to some extent they can still provide a laugh, and more likely a scare. The water system pops out of the ground and turns itself on by a timing system that the passerby knows not of. I have been caught in a car wash of jet streams that suddenly appeared, with the sound of running water the only warning a second before the spray is in the air. We run. In the old days of the moveable sprinklers you could time their circle and outwit their scope. I miss the kerchunk-kerchunk sound of the sprinkler that revolved by its own water power interrupted by a bar on a spring that diverted some water sideways. I miss the clackety-clack of the olden reel movers that were towed by a farm tractor or pushed by hand. The power mowers that speed along with whirling knives create a world less kind.

We throw so much away. Notre Dame is a small city, and we throw so much away. The dining hall used to throw so much food away. Some food was wasted on plates of diners whose eyes were bigger than their stomachs, some food because too much was prepared, and some food by law could not be served once again. Food is now taken to the homeless shelter in downtown South Bend, and as in the gospel story, the hungry are well fed on the twelve baskets of fragments left over from the seven loaves and two fishes that fed "five thousand, not counting the women and children" (Lk 9:14).

We throw away in a world where there is no "away." Everything we put into landfills or garbage dumps goes back into the land and contaminates the water that we must drink tomorrow. The water we run over our lawns picks up the dirt of our smog-filled airs, the fertilizers of our plantings, the tons of chemicals of our winter sidewalks and roads, the detritus of our lives. We send our impurities back into our soil, our rivers, and our lakes. Perhaps there is no other way to live our lives. But I wish it were the other way around. I wish it were like the baptism of Jesus, who entered Jordan's water, not because he needed to be cleansed, but because the waters of baptism needed to be made pure for God's grace. I wish we made our water pure by our use, or used less of what was already pure, or just were more aware of how blessed by God we are in northern Indiana—lands graced with abundant fresh water that, we should remember, is not inexhaustible.

Notre Dame Ballet

WHEN A READER sees the title of this reflection they must be thinking of a staged ballet. The dancers fly through the air with the greatest of ease. Their legs are as supple and expressive as their arms, and their whole body manifests an airy vocabulary. The dancer interprets the music, or interprets space itself, but sing of the body and its glory the dancer must. I could watch classical ballet forever, I think, for it excites my spirit. In wonder at how gravity can be so disregarded, I find that time itself in my soul is suspended, and for the moment I forget myself and my world and look upon an ecstasy of this our mortal flesh. Notre Dame, alas, has no ballet company. However, it does have young men and young women with supple bodies and a gracefulness that will also take your breath away.

Along the open lawns of the campus you can watch students, male and female, throwing a Frisbee, and if you stop to watch you will see from time to time a genuine acrobat climbing the air to make an impossible catch and making it look as sweet as rocking in a hammock. On the sidewalks there is always someone on a skateboard, and from time to time one observes the human body on this broken-bone-trap-on-wheels skying up and down a staircase and along a ledge with nothing to hold their feet on a board that looks slippery as a greased watermelon. It's not ballet, but it will take your breath away and maybe make your heart stop. When I watch varsity women's volleyball I see ballet at Notre Dame. Those young women move quicker than your eye, and they do leaps and dives so astonishing and so impossible that you will come away rubbing your eyes in disbelief.

Along the lake paths the joggers come and go in all sizes and shapes. Many of them spend too much time and energy lifting themselves up and down instead of moving their bodies forward. And then appears a runner whose motion is liquid, whose feet do not touch the ground, whose rhythm was made in heaven, and who glides across the land like a phantom with a swift gracefulness that can hardly be surpassed. One stares in wonder, because it is so clear they are not even trying to run.

Every springtime at Notre Dame when all the natives have cabin fever from the winter weather, there is a basketball tournament. The campus stakes claim to the largest college intramural basketball tournament in the world. About six hundred teams begin the relentless countdown to the final two teams in competition for the campus championship title. The teams are ragtag, often with outrageous names, many with hilarious names, and some with names so gross the school censors them. Rain or shine, snow or heat, the games are played on the asphalt and concrete outdoor courts of Notre Dame. After the first week, half the teams have been eliminated. In the end Domers will watch basketball skills on display that you will not see on the varsity floorboards. It takes a street-smart player to win the student tournament. It takes speed, cleverness, determination, and a miraculous hand that makes baskets when nothing should emerge from such a tangle. It's not classical ballet, but it is modern dance by bodies with athletic skills and grace that compare with diamonds in the rough.

In Tolstoy's *War and Peace* there is a winter party of the young people in the family. Natasha, one of the lovely heroines of the novel, is engaged to be married. On the sleigh ride home under the stars she exclaims that she does not think she will ever again be as happy as she is right now. I think of Notre Dame students. They too may never again be quite as lovely as they are in these college years. There is reason, I believe, for this feeling. Our students are old enough to move with adult grace and accomplishment, and they are young enough to be innocent and playful like a child. It is a rare moment of transition, with one foot in childhood and the other firmly planted in the maturity of adulthood. Collegians blend them both, or better yet they cut a path through the air around them like the twin blades of a scissors designed to bring both sides together precisely. When I see young male and female bodies at play and unaware of their own agile coordination, I think of that moment in aerial trapeze, when the acrobat has let go of the bar that hitherto was their support in gaining the altitude they now enjoy, and they fall through the air in a moment of dazzle and danger before grasping hold of a partner's outstretched hands swinging in synchronization to meet their body in its airy hesitation, and then to lift them into the safety of the future. That moment of free fall can be so daring and so beautiful, and I see it on the lawns of Notre Dame in student playfulness and in the drama of the human heart of young college students on this campus, where so much raw talent is on display.

Reflecting Pool

EVERY SUMMER THAT I can recollect since the construction of the large rectangular reflecting pool on the south side of the Hesburgh Library at Notre Dame, a family of ducks makes its home in these shallow waters. The baby ducks can hardly jump up from the water to the marble ledge of the pool, and compassionate passersby rig up boards to help them. At noontime bemused spectators share their lunch with the ducks, whose belly feathers are proudly colored aquamarine from the algae-reducing chemicals in the pool water. It is at night, however, that one sees the mother duck gather her young in the shadow of her wings. "Be merciful to me, O God, be merciful to me, for in you my soul takes refuge; in the shadow of your wings I will take refuge, until the destroying storms pass by" (Ps 57:1). The ducklings push and shove to find shelter under their mother's wings, and the last one under pushes out the first one in. Finally they all pack themselves under her wings, and the mother bird sits quietly under a bush in her nighttime vigil in defense of those she loves. "Jerusalem, Jerusalem, the city that kills the prophets and stones those who are sent to it! How often have I desired to gather your children together as a hen gathers her brood under her wings, and you were not willing!" (Lk 13:34).

The reflecting pool was designed to capture the image of Christ that dominates the south wall of the library facing the football stadium. The students call this figure of

Christ, with arms upraised and visible above the north-end goal posts from inside the stadium, "Touchdown Jesus." This enormous ten-story mosaic mural is composed of hundreds of pieces of some eighty differing granites, marbles, and other stone taken from countries around the world. At night when the spotlights illumine the figure of Christ against the night sky, the radiance of his presence dominates the campus. He is the beginning and the ending of Truth itself, and the amplitude of the library book collection but reflects his plenitude. Here is God with us. Here is the fullness of truth that the books of the library but seek. "I am the way, and the truth, and the life" (Jn 14:6).

One looks into this pool of clear water and one sees the face of Christ, who is the unique Word of God and the everlasting Truth. He is surrounded in the mural by the sages of Christianity, the saints and the mystics, the philosophers and the theologians, the learned wise men of yesteryear east and west. I say wise men with some sadness, for it is not clear that there are any women represented in this spectacular tribute dedicated to Christian learning leading to the imposing figure of Christ as the summit and consummation of all wisdom. Three women have been proclaimed "doctors of the Church": Saint Catherine of Siena, Saint Teresa of Avila, and most recently Saint Thérèse of Lisieux. Many other women have been learned and wise teachers of the Church. Many are the women saints and mystics who have lived the faith and taught the love of God. Women ought to be reflected in this mural, for in their eyes the Church has so often seen Christ. In the well of wisdom that is womankind, the reflection of Christ also emerges clearly from those waters.

In Dante's *Commedia* the poet sees Christ reflected in the eyes of Beatrice, who looks on Christ with an enraptured love. In this closing scene of the "Purgatorio," set in the Garden of Eden, Christ is represented as a griffin, a mythical creature with the body of a lion and the head of an eagle. The human nature of Christ and the divine nature are symbolized in the poet's imagination. Dante looks into the emerald-green eyes of the woman he has loved all his life and from whom he had wandered. There in her eyes filled with love he sees the griffin that is Christ. She reflects Christ to him, just as the pursuit of truth and wisdom brings us in its reflection a glimpse of the very Word of God, whom we hope to see fully in the eternity of heaven face to face. Would that we could see Christ reflected in the eyes of everyone we meet here and now.

In the story of the unnamed woman who washes the feet of Jesus with her tears and dries them with her hair (Lk 7:36–50), the contemporary translations of the Bible have all made it clear that she is much forgiven, and then she loves much. Her love is a response to love given her, which was experienced as the forgiveness of her sins. She did not find it in herself to first love Jesus, who was thereby moved to forgive her. Jesus loved her and she responded. Our life is a response to God's love. Our life is a reflection of Christ's love that shines in our hearts. Our life is a reflecting pool wherein we see the face of Christ, know the truth of Christ, and receive the love of Christ. Then and only then can we give away to others that wonderful discovery of God's everlasting love that we glimpse in the still waters of our night.

Trees

THE LANDSCAPE AT Notre Dame is so green when the rainfall attains its customary plenitude. One takes the lush vegetation for granted. Whatever its shortcomings, northern Indiana proves a bountiful host for trees. Every variety of tree thrives here. The soil itself is a sandy loam from glacier till that provides deep unobstructed room for tree roots to expand and an underground water supply that would be reliable even in times of drought. The water table is low hereabouts, and the aquifer is enormous. The same glaciers that carved out the Great Lakes, which contain one-fifth of the world's fresh water, left the surrounding lands with bottomless wells and underground rivers of clean water. Frequent lightning storms bring down needed nitrogen from the skies above. The campus of Notre Dame is a paradise for trees.

Even the climate itself welcomes trees. Notre Dame is situated in a narrow belt of land that marks the northernmost reach of many species of warm climate trees of this hemisphere. At the same time the campus enjoys a location that is the southernmost reach of many species of cold climate trees of North America. On top of the favorable circumstances of climate, soil, and water, the campus was befriended by one of the brothers whose avocation was horticulture. Brother Philip Kinze, C.S.C., was long responsible for planting every variety of tree he could find, and he nurtured on this campus trees that were thought impossible to grow in this place. He solicited trees from around the world, and travelers from China and elsewhere brought back tiny specimens for his husbandry. The variety of the trees on campus are a tribute to this one man who planted for future generations to enjoy. Father Peter Hebert, C.S.C., catalogued this abundant variety of flora on the campus, and Notre Dame has published a detailed book describing the trees of Notre Dame and their remarkable quantity and quality.[4]

The sycamore is a native tree of Indiana. An ancient and impressive sycamore tree stands in the lowlands between the Grotto and the lake. Its feet must be in the wet lake level, and its setting in a hollow must have protected it from the worst of storms. It would take four adults linked hand in hand to girdle the circumference of the trunk. In its low saddle where the four trunks branch both children and lovers climb to have their picture taken. Wire cables hold the overextended branches in equilibrium. The sycamore tree has the largest crown of any tree, and this centuries-old sycamore enjoys an upper circumference that is enormous.

The Dutch elm trees at Notre Dame once upon a time shaded the campus walkways and decorated the atmosphere with elaborate laced branches that reached high in the skies. Like the chestnut tree of yesteryear, the Dutch elm has been destroyed by a fungus that has spared hardly a one, and even the survivors remain on borrowed time. Given the thousands of maple trees on this campus, one hopes with

4. Barbara Hellenthall, Thomas Schlereth, and Robert McIntosh, *Trees, Shrubs and Vines on the University of Notre Dame Campus* (University of Notre Dame Press, 1993).

all one's soul that there will never be a maple tree blight that would deprive our eyes of the kaleidoscope of golden fire in the autumn leaf season that yearly delights our souls. And yet we know all our trees are in the hands of God, and Joyce Kilmer was right when in his poem he declared "But only God can make a tree." Gerard Manley Hopkins knew something of the bittersweet reality of our death in life and our life in death when the autumn leaves leave us with such fallen beauty and with an annual reminder of our mortality.

Spring and Fall

Margaret, are you grieving
Over Goldengrove unleaving?
Leaves, like the things of man, you
With your fresh thoughts care for, can you?
Ah! as the heart grow older
It will come to such sights colder
By and by, nor spare a sigh
Though worlds of wanwood leafmeal lie;
And yet you will weep and know why.
Now no matter, child, the name:
Sorrow's springs are the same.
Nor mouth had, no nor mind, expressed
What heart heard of, ghost guessed:
It is the blight man was born for,
It is Margaret you mourn for.

The Peace Fountain

THE STUDENTS CALL it Stonehenge. Some see it as a war memorial. I prefer to look upon it as the peace fountain. Raised up where rested the old Field House that withstood with its low ceiling so many deafening basketball seasons, enormous pillars of limestone framed with a black marble basin now stand in the spray of high gushing waters. The pillars are rough hewn and the blocks of stone supported between them clearly fragmentary pieces of an unfinished building. "Unless the Lord builds the house, those who build it labor in vain. Unless the Lord guards the city, the guard keeps watch in vain" (Ps 127:1).

This fountain of living water is a memorial of the mid-century wars of this country, and its purpose is to keep alive the memory of some five hundred Notre Dame students that gave their lives for the cause of their nation and its people. No war is ever anything but tragic. Perhaps World War II comes closest to a "good" war in the eyes of almost everyone, for in that war an unbridled aggression was opposed and overcome. The Asian conflicts of Korea and of Vietnam have never been so readily resolved in our national conscience. The moral issues were not as clear. What does remain clear is this: Anyone who lays down his or her life has made a statement that carries a credibility and a generosity that nothing can take away. As Lincoln recognized in his poignant address in honor of the many soldiers fallen in the battle of Gettysburg, "The world will little note, nor long remember what we say here, but it can never forget what they did here."

To the east of the peace fountain, the library rises up tall and stark. The stone pillars mimic the overall outline of the library and tie the stonework into a balanced architecture. In the center of the water basin a large ball of red porphyry granite stone gives color to the memorial. Around the edges, coffin-like black marble, low walls retain the flowing waters. The sections are measured short for coffins, too short for lives that were cut down too soon. The porphyry stone is blood colored, and the waters that splash over the globe shaped like planet Earth are washed clean. Hegel said "history was a butcher's block," and surely the twentieth century saw more massive and indiscriminate violence and bloodshed than any century before in human history. The water cascading around the cold and hard stone of the memorial has always seemed to me a most silent and poignant commentary on the human condition. Bodies are not stone. Our bodies are but warm water in fragile envelopes. Our flesh remains vulnerable, and our lives are ever in jeopardy.

Students often lounge around the fountain. They lean against its marble sides and study or sunbathe. Young children often wade in its waters on a warm day. Coins are thrown into the fountain for good luck. War seems far away. Every few months someone in the pursuit of good humor puts a box of soap suds in the fountain and it becomes a sea of foam. The prank has become tedious and the detergent dissolves the oils in the bearings of the water pumps. I wonder—do we play at life? Surely we thoughtlessly play at war. And not all the soap in the world will wash all the blood off our hands. "Out, damned spot" was the cry of Lady Macbeth, and its echo reaches our ears.

On this piece of ground on Notre Dame campus, where the fieldhouse once stood, many were the young men who ran indoor track, and many were the young men who played basketball to the cheer of the packed-in crowds. In later years, as the building was replaced with the new basketball and hockey domes, the fieldhouse became a studio for artists. From a foundry built on the dirt track of yesteryear, molten bronze was poured into beautiful forms. From the melting metal a new and more beautiful artifact appeared. When I think of the wartime lives given up, the incomplete lives, the tragic lives, the seeming waste of young vigor and promise, I would dare to hope that God is the artist who shapes in the fires of our inhumanity to each other the deeper goodness that was trapped inside our intricate hearts and needed only a loving hand to be cast free and prove itself even more beautiful.

Museum Courtyard

THERE ARE NOT many places in the midst of the buildings on the campus of Notre Dame where one can be alone. In the Grotto people are coming and going almost all the time. At the Mestrovic "Woman at the Well" aside O'Shaughnessy Hall a flow of people pass in front. In the Basilica it is rare in the daytime not to find visitors circulating. But there are three courtyards at Notre Dame, and each is quiet. The Brownson Hall courtyard for many years boasted a spectacular flower garden in the summer, which alas has of late gone to seed. But the place is still quiet and out of the way, yet just a few feet from the Dome. The courtyard in Hayes-Healy, the old Commerce Building and School of Business (recently become the home of the Mathematics Department), is hidden in the very center of the two separate buildings that are joined on their perimeter. Rarely have I sat there on the stone benches under the trees that I have not felt alone and in a garden. The saying goes that one is never closer to God than in a garden. My contemplative courtyard, however, is the museum courtyard, which is maintained with beautiful landscaping and adorned with outdoor sculpture. It is an oasis in the middle of the most active classrooms and faculty offices. Attached to the Snite Museum, the courtyard can be entered only through the building itself, where one must pass the many rooms that hold the treasures of art that Notre Dame has been fortunate enough to gather. Not many college museums in our land have a collection as complete from early times to the present, nor as well displayed. I am amazed that I sit alone in the courtyard. Truly it remains a garden of contemplation in the middle of activity. In the center of the garden is a stainless steel metal sculpture by George Rickey. A turbine-shaped fan blade is supported on a pedestal and both the fan and the its support on top of the pedestal twist round and round according to the wind direction and velocity. It cannot be described in words, but the motion is so intriguing and so unpredictable that I have watched in fascination for long periods of time. The Holy Spirit comes as the wind comes, from we know not where, soft as the breeze and strong as the storm, coming and going unpredictably and invisibly, and yet dazzling the face of the earth with its graceful motion and sudden and serendipitous movement in the human heart.

The more the campus is developed with new buildings, sidewalks, and roads the less land is covered with grass and trees. Progress, one supposes, is inevitable, and the university is not designed to be a garden. But thank God there are garden places where we are reminded that we cannot live without beauty. Our souls starve without beauty. We need beauty in our buildings as well. And when all is said and done, it would seem that beauty comes from the artistic arrangement of anything loved enough to be shaped with care and displayed to delight. The museum is a cornucopia of the fruits of artistic endeavors to create beauty in every way, in every medium, in every expression. The artist who tends the museum garden may not have critical reviews, but in this person's view, his or her work is lovely to behold and a place to be with God, to be with one's self, and to share with a friend. The courtyard remains a peaceful, quiet, and beautiful place at Notre Dame to be.

Olden Places

Stadium

Corby Hall Porch

Old College

Holy Cross Hill

North Shore West

North Shore East

Powerplant

Crossroads

Stadium

AS I WRITE this reflection the sun is rising over the library due east of the central campus, and all is quiet on a brisk September morning. In a few hours more than 80,000 people will be milling about peacefully and happy to be in this place. It is a football Saturday and the circus, the parade, the family reunion, the nostalgia trip, the legendary sports event in the house that Rockne built will strike up the band and shake down the thunder from the sky. Not exactly, of course, but close. Football on the Notre Dame campus is secular ritual, and the only event I know that gives a parallel and a similar flavor is the appearance of the pope to the crowd assembled outside in the Vatican piazza. In the one place there is a secular devotion of a body of people tinged with a religious awareness, and in the other a religious devotion tinged with a worldly awareness that the papacy holds together as a people.

The stadium was renovated and expanded in the mid-1990s. An upper deck was cantilevered over the top of the original brick and concrete stadium of 1930. The pieces of reinforced concrete were trucked in preformed and dropped into place by huge cranes deftly as a child might snap lego pieces together. The original stadium cost less than a million dollars and will stand far in the future. It was a respectful decision to save it and not to build a bigger and newer stadium in the woodland north of the university campus. The expansion that added twenty thousand seats to the sixty thousand in place cost almost fifty million dollars. Not that the football fans would not pay for those seats and pay for them in short order. What seemed extravagant was so many dollars for a structure that is used eighteen hours a year. And yet, who can say what meaning and what joy is brought to the half-million people who every autumn will flood the campus of Notre Dame to visit their friends, pray at sacred places, relive old memories, and watch a football game that is just a game but that touches loyalties as simple as that of a subway alum to that of pride in being Catholic in a nation that was not always proud of having Catholics in its midst.

Notre Dame owes a great deal to football. It gave the school a national reputation. It brought an alumni loyalty that is the envy of all academia, and a following of "alums" that includes many folks who never walked the campus of Notre Dame. With the reputation and the publicity came many of the other necessities of a growing and ambitious university. Knute Rockne was at the heart of the legend of college football and indeed of football as a national sport. That he died young in a plane crash caused by bad weather in the years when airplanes were less prepared to deal with the elements is one of the tragedies that still lingers in the heart of Notre Dame. That is why keeping the old stadium intact seems so right. The new cradles the old, much like the new moon with the old moon in its arms. In Rome there is a Renaissance church dedicated to Saint Clement, which was built on top of the leveled-off ruins of a Romanesque church of medieval times, itself on top of the ruins of a pagan temple. Excavations have restored the original pavement of imperial Rome and restored the simple beauty of the Romanesque church. Our past, whether in our people or in our architecture, should not be casually abandoned.

There is an aesthetic joy in sports, and there is a athleticism in top-rate football that can take your breath away. Spectator participation varies from the fan who can appreciate the impossible catch to those who recognize the strategy of the game that cannot readily be seen. It is said that football builds character in its players. No doubt it has given courage, loyalty, and perseverance to many a young man. At the same time, one sees in the very competitive football of today an aggressiveness that may pose moral problems for players trained to win at any cost. All too many football stars make the newspapers because of violence off the field, and one may wonder if they bring the violence to their football practice or whether they take violence away as a lesson of how one prevails. Notre Dame has always tried to be wholesome and respectful of the integral education of its athletes. As with liberty, eternal vigilance is the price of integrity.

I am not a football fan who attends every game and waves the flag. It hurts too much when they lose. At times I attend the game for only the first half, when sitting on the hard bench I suffer a backache, and from the loudspeakers in my ear a headache, and from the play on the field a heartache. "Why am I doing this?" I say. Alas, not much fan loyalty in this fair-weather friend. And yet, I love Notre Dame football for its people and for its dreams. Where would Notre Dame be without it? What would the university be without the family of Notre Dame that gathers so often to watch grown men chase an inflated pigskin?

Corby Hall Porch

ON THE FRONT porch of Corby Hall, where the priests and brothers have their meals and a part of the Holy Cross community has residence, there is a row of rocking chairs that appears when the weather warms in the spring. Every once and a while in the middle of the night one of the rockers walks away. Then the word goes out to the maids in the dorms to keep an eye out for a Corby rocker. Chairs reappear as miraculously as they disappear. These chairs are Kennedy rockers, the chair designed for President Kennedy to ease his back pains. I never sit down in one of these rockers without thinking of him and where I was the day he was shot to death. Memories of Camelot tease my mind, and I sometimes think of the humorous, half-serious description of Notre Dame as the Catholic Disneyland—a spiritual ride of one kind or another for everyone. Notre Dame does cherish a dream, just as the Kennedy era generated a dream, just as the gospel tells of humankind's hopeful dream of the Kingdom of God on Earth. We want here a piece of that dream.

After supper the brethren rock together on the porch. Behind us are the yellow handmade bricks of the facade of this old building. The brothers of Holy Cross made the bricks, and the students who long ago lived in this building preserved a custom of writing on one of these bricks their name, perhaps their town, and the date of their graduation. The carbon in pencil lead does not erode easily, and the porch roof protected the bricks from the weather. I would read with nostalgia the names on these bricks going back to the beginning of this century. It was comforting to have them with us and behind our efforts. They were our alumni, living or dead, our communion of saints, the living stones of this university much as the faithful remain the living stones of the church. One of my students told me that she walked through the Basilica at a lonely moment and was comforted by the saints depicted in the stained glass windows. To her they seemed to be great grandparents. It was family, and she was not alone. Alas, the names on the bricks of Corby Hall porch were recently erased when the whole building exterior was cleaned. The bricks shine now, and though the names are gone to my eyes, I know each brick represents someone's efforts to be among the saints of Notre Dame.

From the front porch of Corby Hall, as one looks out and rocks in peaceful leisure, the face of change is all around. The renovated architecture building so classical and elegant was the university library when I was a student. The old worn steps are gone, but I hope not the echo of our footsteps. Howard Hall now houses young women, and Badin Hall as well. The old bookstore in the basement of Badin is long gone, but so is the new bookstore that rose up in the beginning of the Hesburgh era some fifty years ago. Campus ministry and the First Year of Studies share the new magnificent facilities in the neo-Gothic Colman-Morse building. The old post office is gone and the Knights of Columbus occupy the little Gothic building to the east of the old bookstore. Walsh Hall is a residence for women students now, and Sorin Hall, which completes the view from the porch, is the residence of Father Malloy, the president of the university succeeding Father Hesburgh. The old elms are gone and the old asphalt sidewalks. But one still looks out on the many hopeful faces cherishing the dream of Notre Dame.

The elderly and retired of the Holy Cross university community tend to live in Corby Hall. One could argue, however, that priests and brothers never retire. They work at being educators in the faith no matter how few hours their health may allow. One never just rocks on the porch. Our vocation is to work freely and without counting cost. One is never retired, because one is always available free of charge. One's life belongs to the Christian community. We are a nonprofit community at Notre Dame. One might argue that all the caregivers in society, from politicians to doctors to teachers to ministers, ought not become rich in serving the compelling needs of the body of Christ. We all should work for nothing; we should work for the love of God. That would clearly make our life a God-given vocation. Of course, one has expenses and they should be met. A religious community must educate the young and take care of the infirm and the sick. A family must do the same and needs to count raising children and later years of retirement into its expenses. Everyone need vacations and a decent home with leisure and amenities. It is said that George Washington took no salary while president of the United States, but he did enjoy a generous expense account. And rightly so. But rich from the ineluctable needs of others we are not. And retired we are not. We hope our health allows us to serve in some way, even if only to pray and to rock on the porch and smile upon the visitor who ascends the porch steps and may come to feel they are included in the family of Notre Dame, a family made up finally of its people and not its bricks.

Old College

MORE THAN ANY other place on the campus of Notre Dame, I like to sit on a bench by the Old College and the Log Chapel, on the path lined by old maple trees and overlooking Saint Mary's Lake. I often come here in the morning with a cup of hot coffee to sit and pray before going to morning prayer in Corby Hall Chapel. The lake is quiet. A few strollers and several joggers are circling the path around the lake. The ducks and geese come and go. Occasionally the swans take to the air with a flap of spray and wings and circle the lake once or twice beating the air with feathers that whir almost like a windmill.

A few yards along the sidewalk sits Old College, the original building of Notre Dame. When it was built in 1842 this "university" was hardly more than a grammar school together with a few advanced students who might continue their education. To come to this wilderness of Indiana and to dream of a university of Our Lady was a consummate act of hope and trust in God.

I sit here to pray because almost fifty years ago I sat here and decided that I might have a vocation to the priesthood and to the Congregation of Holy Cross. When, in a Benedictine prep school in New Jersey, I had given thought to entering the monastery. But it seemed not yet. Then I came to Notre Dame, and I thought if the desire was again aroused here, how else would God tell me that I might belong here at Notre Dame? It was after I came back from a date with a Saint Mary's student that the question seemed to clarify. We had gone to see Marlon Brando in *A Streetcar Named Desire*. I kept thinking about desire and what my heart's desire was, and whether or not anything or anyone in this world could satisfy the deep desires that kept me restless. I walked the shore of the lake in front of Old College, and I think the grace of God brought me to enter the seminary program for collegians, which it turned out by providence was housed in the Old College. It proved a good place to test a vocation that was itself a risk and a commitment, much like the founding of Notre Dame. The outcome was not clear. One would have to leave home. The road not taken would always be at the back of one's mind. God's grace and Our Lady's protection should be ever at the heart of this endeavor if it were to bear fruit.

In this old brick ramshackle building more than a dozen of us lived with a Holy Cross priest, who loved us dearly. Father Jerry Wilson, C.S.C., was himself a late vocation, and one sensed how much he had finally found what all his life he had been looking for. Old College became a spiritual home and not just a roof over my head. The Log Chapel was our chapel, and we spent Saturday afternoons waxing the wooden floor on our hands and knees. It seemed pioneer and missionary, for the labor of many hands built Notre Dame when only forest and empty field lay before those first brothers. Father Sorin stood on this site and dreamed of building a seminary for Christian life for the lay students of a continent who would come here to find their vocation in the world.

Outside Old College to this day there is a hand pump that brings up water from the well that provided the drinking water in the beginning days for the community at Notre Dame du Lac. In my day it still worked, and the water was cool and pure. I remember how the pump often needed to be primed, as we all need to be encouraged. I remember how it squeaked, because its moving parts were old, as we all will become. I think now of the account in John's gospel of the woman at Jacob's well (chapter 4). For hundreds of years the people of God had drunk from that well, their families and their flocks. She came with her jug to draw water, and Jesus asked her to give him a drink. He offered her in exchange a fountain of living water welling up in her heart, if only she would receive the grace of God and come to know him who was gifting her. She had five husbands, Jesus tells her, and none of them had quenched her thirst. "Sir," she said, "I see that you are a prophet" (Jn 4:19). Then she believed and she received the waters of grace. She left her jug, which comprised all her former way of satisfying the thirsts of her life, and she became an apostle of Jesus to the people of her village. And so had Father Sorin and the brothers of Holy Cross who built the Old College. And so perhaps could I.

Holy Cross Hill

ALONG THE ROAD from the Grotto to Saint Mary's College on a hilltop overlooking Saint Mary's Lake stood Holy Cross Seminary for a century. In its last years this venerable building housed Notre Dame students. It proved to be too expensive to renovate, and the decision to raze the building brought it down in a matter of days. The original building was of solid brick, thick-wall construction. Its chapel had wooden ceiling beams that reminded me of a medieval Romanesque church. Unlike buildings that are held together with steel beams and reinforced concrete, when these walls were rocked the whole structure collapsed with a cloud of dust. Soon it was gone in trucks to a landfill out of sight, and a grassy knoll emerged with an unimpeded view of the Basilica and the main campus across the east end of the lake. The ground is sacred to me because of the seminary which sowed seeds of grace on this spot in the hearts of men. That seed of God's love lingers in the ground, and I cannot walk by Holy Cross Hill without a memory of those unnamed many. I believe that their spirits are not altogether absent from this holy ground. I believe in the communion of saints.

When I cannot sleep at night or wake up in the middle of the darkness, I often say my rosary. When that prayer will not put me to sleep I call upon all those whom I have known and loved and who are now in eternal life before the face of God. I call them by name, and I ask them to come and sit all around the sides of my bed. I call upon Jesus and Mary and Joseph, my parents, and their parents, and my list can be very long. I picture them as I would picture the people who once dwelt on Holy Cross Hill. I know they are real and that they live and that our spirits are in communion. I believe in the communion of saints—not ghosts, but saints in heaven. I believe in the resurrection of our bodies and life everlasting. I sleep in good company.

My only experience in Holy Cross Seminary consists of a Latin class taught to me there as a seminarian living at that time in Moreau Seminary on Saint Joseph's Lake. A happy priest taught a number of us remedial Latin, for we had not attended the high school seminary that stood on Holy Cross Hill. He was a dear man who taught us little Latin but loved us well. I never thought I would need much Latin, but when I graduated from Notre Dame I was sent to study theology in Rome, where classes were taught in Latin and oral examinations were conducted in Latin. Thrown in the water I learned to swim and even to swim well. Holy Cross Hill comes back to me with a smile in my heart. One never knows what God has in mind down the road.

One small thing was spared on Holy Cross Hill and remains radiant in place to this day. A small statue of Saint Thérèse of Lisieux is situated on the south face of the hill. She is tucked in among the trees and bushes that surround her. Seminarians in the fifties owned a devotion to her "little way," which taught that sanctity was found in the doings of ordinary life done with great love for God. They scraped together donations to buy a little statue of the beloved saint Thérèse, and with their own hands they laid the foundation. Over the years I have always seen flowers planted at her feet. Someone was tending the shrine of Saint Thérèse long after Holy Cross Hill was vacant and abandoned. I found out it was the priest who was the procurator of Holy Cross foreign missions. Though a cloistered Carmelite nun, Thérèse had always wanted to be a missionary and to die a martyr for the sowing of the seed of the faith in a land far away. All she could do was pray for the foreign missions, and we know conversion is always a matter of God's grace and not primarily our own endeavors. When Thérèse was canonized a saint, she was also made the patron of the foreign missions in the Church.

One of our younger Holy Cross priests has planted a number of seedling trees on the top of Holy Cross Hill. He waters them by hand in the summer and tends them with hope in the future. As the humorous line goes, the elderly do not buy green bananas. It takes faith to plant a tree whose fulfillment one may never live to see. It takes faith to believe that vocations to the mission of the Church will grow and flourish in the hearts of young women and men. It takes faith to believe that the word of God will be received in the hearts of those who have heretofore never heard it, because it was never preached to them. I never walk around the lake path and pass Holy Cross Hill without feeling in my bones the spirit of God that hovers over this place, and over all our hearts if we have faith to see. We have hope that were our faith like a tiny mustard seed it is promised us in God's providence to prosper into a large bush where the birds of the air would find refuge.

North Shore West

THE NORTH SHORE of Saint Joseph's Lake belongs to the Congregation of Holy Cross, and three of its buildings stand on its edges. In the center the dominant architecture is the current Moreau Seminary, a building of the 1950s but constructed with curving lines that wrap around the central chapel building so that the eye never tires of looking at its complexity. Seminarians, myself included, were involved in its design, and the architects took to heart many of the suggestions we made. The curved corridors were a seminarian suggestion to avoid the dismal long straight dark corridor effect of a big building. Many sources of natural light were built into walls and ceilings. The library floor beneath the chapel includes curved platforms, which gives variety to an otherwise rectangular space. The covered outdoor walkway was designed so the residents could recite the divine office while walking outside even with inclement weather. The south wall of the chapel facing the lake is one huge panel of stained glass, magnificent in its color and design, depicting the angels that surround the altar of sacrifice. The seminary was built to accommodate two hundred seminarians at a time when the old seminary slightly to the west was overcrowded with eighty-eight seminarians, an all-time high for Holy Cross vocations. The plans of mice and men often go astray. Vocations to the priesthood and brotherhood never reached that plateau again and have been in a steady decline to a level much more modest indeed.

To the west of the present seminary in its largesse stands the old seminary of the old yellow brick, a rectangular box-like structure built by the Indiana Province as their college seminary. I lived three years in this building, and all the seminarians studied philosophy and Latin in preparation for the theological studies that would lead to priestly ordination. The brothers followed a program more appropriate to their future apostolates. We were crowded and we were poor. Orange crates and surplus army double-decker bunks and blankets were the furniture of the day. If one had business in downtown South Bend, one was given one bus token and could choose to walk to town or walk back. Our day was completely regulated by a disciplined schedule that provided ample time for prayer, for study, for sleep, for meals, for recreation both indoor and outdoor, and for every community event. Occasionally the hand bell was rung to signal a break time in our study hours and smoking was then allowed. People rolled their own cigarettes from loose tobacco. Most everyone smoked in chains when the smoking was permitted. A few of us who did not smoke lobbied for hot chocolate, but we suffered the fate of most minorities. Strange as this monastic world was, I must say I was happy, perhaps the most happy that I have ever been. We were living in the early days of our vocation and love for God. There was never a worry or concern about how we would manage our time and our obligations. We had but to live the communal life, accept the manifest will of God, and attend to the God within. What Benedict wanted in founding Western monasticism I think I understood. Peace within and peace without.

Gone are the days of this older Moreau Seminary. Gone are the chicken sheds and the feather-plucking parties when we prepared for Sunday dinner those chickens who because of age or illness no longer were laying eggs. Gone is old Kaiser the plow horse, who when he fell down we had to pry up with boards to put him again on his feet. Gone is the "yellow peril," the broken-down school bus that carried us to summer camp and overheated or somehow failed in crossing through the traffic of Chicago in the days before there were freeways.

When the new seminary was built, the old one became Saint Joseph Hall, a residence for collegian seminarians prior to the novitiate and subsequently for graduate students. The building now has been renovated and beautifully adapted as a parish center for Sacred Heart Parish and as a residential facility for campus retreats and special housing needs. If the walls could talk they would have much to say, much to laugh about, and some things to cry over. In the end we are all are so blessed with our faith, our Lord Jesus, and the vocation from God that every one of us enjoys. When you walk by the seminary, the old and the new, remember that God calls you in baptism to holiness and that the University of Notre Dame has been for thousands of young men and young women a "seminary" where they learned something about how the Christian life might be lived in prayer, in community, and in living service of those in need within and beyond this campus.

North Shore East

TO THE EAST and capping the gentle curve of the north shore of Saint Joseph's Lake stands Holy Cross House. Holy Cross priests and brothers who need assisted living or require medical care dwell here. At the turn of the twentieth century it was the novitiate, which was outgrown and moved to Rolling Prairie, Indiana; then to the Hoffman estate in South Bend; then to Jordan, Minnesota; Bennington, Vermont; and now Cascade, Colorado. With adaptations the building became an infirmary. In the 1950s a modern health-care facility was constructed on the site, and at the end of the century a complete renovation brought about the present medical facility and religious house, designed to make the most of the view of the lake and the golden Dome. It is home and comfort for so many religious who have loved Notre Dame. Because so much green insulated glass has been used as wall, Holy Cross House is sometimes called the "Greenhouse." One might think the seminary ought to be the greenhouse, for "seminary" is derived from the Latin word for seed (*semen*), and new vocations are sheltered where they may grow a strong root system before being transplanted into the world. But old age and dying are also the seeds of eternal life. The Church celebrates the day of death as the feast day of the saints, for it was on this day that they were born into eternal life. In truth the Greenhouse is a greenhouse and seminary for everlasting life.

In the parable of the vineyard workers (Mt 20:1–16), Jesus tells of a generous landowner who goes out at the various hours of the day and hires the workers who stand idle in the marketplace. At the end of the day each worker receives the agreed upon daily wage, beginning with those who worked but a little time and ending with those who bore the heat of a long day. I like to think we are all called into God's vineyard, and at the end we all will receive the promised reward, life eternal in heaven in the loving presence of our Lord Jesus Christ together with the Father and the Holy Spirit, and surrounded by the saints in glory. Some of us live long. Brother Cosmas lived on campus to be ninety-nine years old. Others in Holy Cross die young. I think of Father Jim Sullivan, who died of a brain tumor when his advance schooling had just been completed; of Father Bill Toohey, director of campus ministry at Notre Dame, who died suddenly of encephalitis in his best years; of Father Michael McCafferty, law professor at Notre Dame, who died of cancer in the prime of his career; of Father Tom Oddo, the young president of the University of Portland, who died in a car accident.

We know that we are all in the hands of God and we all look forward to the same heaven. Saint Paul wrote: "Christ will be exalted now as always in my body, whether by life or by death. For to me, living is Christ and dying is gain. If I am to live in the flesh, that means fruitful labor for me; and I do not know which I prefer. I am hard pressed between the two: my desire is to depart and be with Christ, for that is far better; but to remain in the flesh is more necessary for you" (Phil 1:20–24). God only knows why we live the years we are given. The parable of the workers in the vineyard reminds us that God's ways are not our ways. God is never stingy; we are, and all too often we make God in our image. God is ever generous, but we are not. God is lavish and prodigal in giving life and heavenly reward to those who labor long years and to those who know but few years. And who among us would want to choose how many will be our days?

Whenever I walk by Holy Cross House on the lakeside I know that Jesus died on the holy cross for each one of us and that God's love is housed in our hearts, however feeble they may be. Our God is infinitely resourceful. We should have hope in this green house, this planet Earth, this human life that the Son of God took to himself in the self-gift of the enfleshment of Jesus of Nazareth. Therefore we await with confidence and with gratitude the salvation of this world and our passage from this life into the next. Saint Paul announces to us such hope:

> I consider that the sufferings of this present time are not worth comparing with the glory about to be revealed to us. For the creation waits with eager longing for the revealing of the children of God; for the creation was subjected to futility, not of its own will but by the will of the one who subjected it, in hope that the creation itself will be set free from its bondage to decay and will obtain the freedom of the glory of the children of God. We know that the whole creation has been groaning in labor pains until now; and not only the creation, but we ourselves, who have the first fruits of the Spirit, groan inwardly while we wait for adoption, the redemption of our bodies. For in hope we were saved. Now hope that is seen is not hope. For who hopes for what is seen? But if we hope for what we do not see, we wait for it with patience. (Rom 8:18–25)

Powerplant

THE SKYLINE OF the Notre Dame campus is punctuated by the Basilica steeple, the golden Dome, and the smokestacks and water tower of the powerplant on the southeast shores of Saint Joseph's Lake. I never pass the powerplant without an awareness of how fragile our life is. Just as we depend on our heart to pump life-giving blood throughout our body, so we depend on electricity to sustain our campus life. Without electricity our situation is critical. Water supplies depend on electric pumps to raise water from the artesian wells to the water tower. The furnaces burn oil, gas, or coal, according to which fuel is currently most economical. Without electricity none of the motors, remote control valves, and computer monitoring would be possible. Notre Dame produces steam for the generation of electricity and the spent steam is then reused in the heating system that reaches through tunnels all parts of the campus. But should the power plant shut down, the campus would be in danger. Food that depends on refrigeration would be lost. Vehicles that depend for fuel on gasoline pumps would run dry. Lights would go out, the winter cold would surround us, and the necessities of life as we know them would be in jeopardy.

In the spring of 1999 the cooling towers burned to the ground. Those fan-driven towers control the heat exchange derived from the waters of the lake that bubble up at the east end from springs that perpetually supply both lakes with fresh water. No cause for the powerplant fire at Notre Dame was ever discovered, and while sabotage is a far-fetched explanation, our world is so interconnected with fallible technology that one feels not more safe the more complicated and wonderful it becomes, but somehow a bit less secure. We know, of course, that emergency generators or furnaces or fans can be brought in on flatbed trucks. Repairs can be made to whatever damage. Portable air conditioning towers were rented, and a limited air-conditioning of campus buildings was secured. Suddenly one recognizes that many buildings have no windows that open. Electric blowers circulate the air. Suddenly one sees how vulnerable we are to electric technology. Suppose the electricity to a wider area of the country went down. Vehicular traffic that carries repair parts and carries our food would be curtailed. And suppose our heart stopped beating. It won't happen, but it could happen. And it is not being pessimistic to remind oneself that life is fragile and that every day we live without pain and in the enjoyment of this beautiful world is a blessing of incalculable worth.

Finally, our heat in the winter and our cooling in the summer in this a city of thousands cost our environment. Even with environmental responsibility and sensitivity, life seems to cost someone something. It would seem a law of nature that we live at the expense of some living creature, whether animal or vegetable. Something must die that something must live. The cold waters of the lakes at Notre Dame are warmed by the heat exchange from the lake. Great are the financial savings and considerable the fossil fuels that need not be expended for the same outcome. And yet the lake has to be chemically monitored or the algae will be out of control, and the fish are always hungry, and not all of them can adjust to warmer water. Huge coal piles on the northern fringe of the campus ensure that the powerplant can weather any short-term shortages or interruption in deliveries of fuel. But coal burning, even with the best smoke-stack scrubbers and technology, seems to leave a sulfur residue in the air that settles in an acid rain downwind that has devastated the lakes and forests of northeastern states. We live, it would seem, always at someone's expense, and someone dies to give us life. It is an awareness not meant to be pessimistic, just as knowing our life remains vulnerable is not meant to make us sad. It should make us immensely humbled and fully aware of what treasures we have been given by God, who in Jesus on the cross died for us and whose divine life we hold as a treasure in earthen vessels.

Crossroads

MANY OF THE roads throughout the campus have at the close of the century received for the first time names. Holy Cross Drive from entrance to entrance, from north to south of the campus grounds and from the east to west, meanders its sinuous way through the heart of the university. Moose Krause Drive runs by the stadium for a short space and gives honor to a man who did so much for the athletic tradition at Notre Dame, both as player and as administrator. Wilson Drive, which runs by the graduate student housing, commemorates the financial vice president under Father Hesburgh for many years; he was a gentle man who saw Notre Dame through stringent financial times. Corby Drive winds up from the lake shore past the front of Corby Hall. There is, however, only one public crossroads on the campus of Notre Dame. Many campus roads intersect, but only at Juniper Road and Douglas Road do public streets crisscross through the lands of Notre Dame. At that intersection there is a large black marble marker, erected at the sesquicentennial anniversary to commemorate the founding of the University of Notre Dame by the Congregation of Holy Cross in the year 1842.

Juniper Road runs north and south through the heart of the campus. It used to be a straight road that ran between Breen-Phillips Hall and the Notre Dame television station, now the Center for Social Concerns. The road ran to the immediate east of O'Shaughnessy Hall and to the west of the football stadium. To the east of Juniper Road there was little construction then. The Navy Drill Hall stood on the edge of the campus before it was torn down to make way for the Hesburgh Library. Married student housing for the returning G.I.s also dotted that landscape with surplus army barracks. Vetville, as it was called, was also razed when its purpose was completed. Juniper Road itself was moved on a gentle curve far to the east of the campus. So expansive has been campus building, however, that Juniper Road now runs between the main campus and graduate student housing, several recreational centers, and the Joyce Center.

Crossing the road always reminds me that the business of the university is not isolated from the business of the city. Town and gown issues are sometimes problematical. The university is a city unto itself in some ways, and in other ways its people benefit from the amenities of the South Bend area in incalculable ways. At the same time the influence of Notre Dame, the largest employer in the area and a source of cultural, intellectual, and spiritual enrichment for the surrounding area, cannot be gainsaid. The charge spoken to Notre Dame students every graduation is not an idle one. They are to turn learning into service. Knowledge should lead to love, and knowing the truth to doing the good.

I look on our crossroads and think of how our lives cross, how the Church and the world must crisscross, how body and soul must intersect, how truth and goodness must commingle, and how the university and the Congregation of Holy Cross must continue to cross paths and to give life each to the other.

Douglas Road was an unpaved cinder road when I came as a student here in 1951. It was a private road that was closed each year for a period of time to preserve university ownership. So heavy was the traffic on Douglas Road that maintenance became a burden. There was also no easy public east-west access across Notre Dame. And thus in time Douglas Road became a road that belonged to the people, who came so often to use it and to need it. By "eminent domain" the county took over the road as its own, and where it crosses Juniper Road, Douglas Road became the public crossroads of Notre Dame.

Notre Dame belonged to the founding Congregation of Holy Cross, but it never belonged to them to sell or to abuse. It was a gift from the beginning, supported by the labors and gifts of many benefactors over the years besides the generous lives of Holy Cross religious. Most of all, Holy Cross was its caretaker, as we are God's caretakers of planet Earth. The land does not belong to us to use for whatever purpose. People need to cross our land and to be enfolded in our university, and Notre Dame belongs to its people by eminent domain. The twenty-first century will see a Notre Dame with lay leadership within the university along with a continued and important presence of the Congregation of Holy Cross. It is said of the Holy Cross religious at Notre Dame that their blood is in the bricks, and that the religious order that founded the university and contributed its animation for so many decades represents the heart and soul of the campus. In some ways the religious community is the continuity of the university's mission, which cannot easily be embodied in individual people, who of necessity must come and go. In sum, the university remains a crossroads of the secular and the sacred, of reason and faith, of time and eternity. And in the end Notre Dame belongs to God, to Country, and to Church—the people of God.

Commemorative Places

Father Sorin

Madonnas

Saint Joseph

Sacred Heart

Corby at Gettysburg

The Woman at the Well

Moses

Saint Ann

Saint Edward

Orestes Brownson

Saint Jude

Father Sorin

AT THE ENTRANCE of the beautifully landscaped apron in front of the Dome Building stands a bronze statue of Father Edward Sorin, C.S.C., the founder of the University of Notre Dame. The students calls this area the "God quad," because the Basilica with its cross-topped steeple and the Dome with Our Lady cover this area with their shadow. Carved in the marble of the pedestal of Father Sorin's monumental statue are these words:

> D.O.M.[5] This monument [stands] in memory of Edward Sorin, Superior General of the Congregation of Holy Cross, founder of the University of Notre Dame, who was conspicuous in apostolic virtues and most studious for Catholic education. Born Feb 8, 1814, he lived to the age of 79. [His] disciples, alumni, and friends erected here [this monument] as a token of [their] veneration and gratitude in the year 1905.

In the beginning when Father Sorin and the band of Holy Cross brothers came to this land, the Log Chapel was the only building. What is now Old College was erected as the first

5. *Dominus Optimus Maximus*, which means "The Lord Best and Sovereign," or more literally "The Lord Optimal and Maximal." This phrase was often found in Christian cemeteries as an acknowledgment of the sovereignty of God in life and in death.

building and the whole college of Notre Dame in its infancy. At that spot Father Sorin stood on a December day in 1842 and wrote to the Very Reverend Basil Mary Moreau, C.S.C., the founder of the Congregation of Holy Cross, the following letter which can be found on a plaque at the site today:

> When we least dreamed of it, we were offered an excellent piece of property, about 640 acres in extent. This land is located in the county of Saint Joseph on the branch of the Saint Joseph river, not far from the city of Saint Joseph [Michigan]. It is a delightfully quiet place, about twenty minutes from South Bend. This attractive spot has taken from the lake which surrounds it the beautiful name of Notre Dame du Lac. . . . It is from here that I write you now.
>
> Everything was frozen over, yet it all seemed so beautiful. The lake, especially, with its broad carpet of dazzling white snow, quite naturally reminded us of the spotless purity of our august Lady whose name it bears, and also of the purity of soul that should mark the new inhabitants of this chosen spot. . . . We were in a hurry to enjoy all the scenery along the lake shore of which we had heard so much. Though it was quite cold, we went to the very end of the lake, and like children came back fascinated with the marvelous beauties of our new home. . . . Once more we felt Providence had been good to us and we blessed God from the depths of our soul.
>
> Will you permit me, dear Father, to share with you a preoccupation which gives me no rest? Briefly, it is this: Notre Dame du Lac was given us by the bishop only on condition that we establish here a college at the earliest opportunity. As there is no other school within more than

> a hundred miles, this college cannot fail to succeed. . . . Before long, it will develop on a large scale. . . . It will be one of the most powerful means for good in this country.
>
> Finally, dear Father, you cannot help see that this new branch of your family is destined to grow under the protection of Our Lady of the Lake and Saint Joseph. At least this is my deep conviction. Time will tell if I am wrong.

Time passed, and Father Sorin was proved right. The university was blessed and it became what it is today, a great Catholic university of international scope.

The son of the famed architect Sir Christopher Wren drafted a line for the tombstone of his father à propos of those great men who were builders. "*Si monumentum vis, circumspice*!" In translation, "if you would wish a monument, look around." To take the measure of Father Edward Sorin one need only look at the magnificent Gothic Basilica of the Sacred Heart (recently restored and newly appointed to look its best). This magnificent structure was built when the land was mostly corn fields and the Indian population still prevailed. In 1870 when the cornerstone was laid, no comparable church was to be found in a territory still pioneer. Its architecture and its accomplishment by a college whose tuition barely covered annual operating expenses was an act of heroic hope in God's providence and the destiny of Notre Dame. To take the measure of Father Edward Sorin one need only look at the Dome Building, the predecessor of which burnt down in 1879, and recall that the present structure rose phoenix-like from the ashes in one summer of heroic workmanship driven by the indomitable will and trust in God of the founder of Notre Dame, who could never be dissuaded that here was God's work, and here was a sacred land set aside for greatness in the plans of divine providence.

I worry not at all about the building of Notre Dame. It lacks no brick and mortar endeavor. Fame and fortune and the manifest blessings of God have come to the university. But I do worry about the soul of Notre Dame. That cannot be built even with stones raised from ashes. The vision of Father Sorin contained in that early letter suggested that "purity of heart" on the part of the "inhabitants of this chosen spot" would always be the touchstone to Notre Dame that matters most in the eternal sight of God. That soul of Notre Dame, holy and Catholic, would be the best monument of all to its founder on Earth and its Lady in heaven.

Madonnas

NOTRE DAME IS distinctive in appearance most of all because of the golden Dome of the main building and the golden statue of Our Lady who watches over the campus. On a sunny day the *alma mater* song, written for the funeral mass of Knute Rockne, catches the scene just right: "proudly in the heavens gleams thy gold and blue. Glory's mantle cloaks thee, golden is thy fame, and our hearts forever, praise thee Notre Dame, and our hearts forever, love thee Notre Dame." Beside the Dome madonna, however, many are the statues of Mary, the mother of God, at Notre Dame. From almost anywhere in the Basilica of the Sacred Heart, the madonna and child in the Lady Chapel draws all eyes to herself lifted up and spotlighted. In the crypt of the church there is a lovely, large, carved wooden madonna of the Immaculate Heart of Mary. The madonna of the Grotto replicates the Grotto of Lourdes, where Bernadette gave a description of a lady dressed in white, with a blue sash, who told her of the mystery of the Immaculate Conception. That revelation was defined as doctrine by the Church in the mid-nineteenth century, when Notre Dame was but in its own youth. A statue of Our Lady crowned queen of heaven stands high in a niche above the entrance to Corby Hall.

There are so many madonnas at Notre Dame. Without exception, every one of the twenty-five student residence halls displays a chapel madonna, many of them modern sculptures done with elegance and feeling, no two quite alike. I think of the very simple wooden madonna in Pangborn Hall chapel, and my heart is joyful even in the memory. I think of the Convent madonna, which for years stood in the courtyard of Brownson Hall, which had been from the beginning to more recent times the convent of the sisters of Holy Cross who did the cooking, the laundry, and prayed so tirelessly for the University of Notre Dame. On a stone pedestal between Zahm and Cavanuagh Halls that statue of Mary crowned with flowers and her feet upon the crescent moon (as we read in Rev 12) and her heel crushing the serpent that misled Eve into sin (as we read in Gen 3) now stands. It bears comparison with the Dome madonna. Most hidden of all the madonnas is surely Our Lady of the Rosary in the little-used lawns behind Carroll Hall on the western fringe of the campus. At the entrance to the university a simple and elegant, even regal madonna stands in the circle at the end of Notre Dame Avenue. It was carved in limestone, but was badly damaged when a drunk driver crashed into the pedestal and broke the statue. Repaired as new it now stands at the entrance to the De Bartolo classroom building, and a bronze reproduction of the statue was erected in its place in the entrance circle.

Called the century of Mary, the years from the definition of the Immaculate Conception in 1854 to the proclamation of the Assumption of Mary, body and soul, into heaven in 1950, devotion to Mary often characterized Catholicism. In Dante's "Purgatorio," Buonconte of Montefeltro (a name reminiscent of one of Notre Dame's football greats) is saved at the last minute of his life because he says but the word Mary in his heart (Canto V:88–109). Mary was the mother of mercy in the times in the Church when the judgment of God seemed not that of unconditional love but that of divine justice. In our own times, we have an image of God as merciful, as the father of the prodigal son, as a God of love. In the apparitions of Mary in the twentieth century dire were her warnings of the judgment to come. Perhaps the role of Mary completes in the hearts of the faithful the side of God that has been lost in the shadows.

Something has changed about the reception of the name of Mary. Prayer to Mary is not as often heard on our lips. Perhaps we pray more directly now to Jesus, who has become the Sacred Heart in our midst. We no longer fear the *pantocrator* judge of the icons of old. It is not that devotion to Mary at the Grotto of Notre Dame diminishes, but perhaps her name is not first on our lips. In the Christian scriptures no name is more common than Mary. In the gospels: Mary of Nazareth, Mary of Magdala, Mary of Bethany, Mary the wife of Clopas, and so forth. Not long ago many were the students whose name was Mary. The founder of the Congregation of Holy Cross was called Basil Anthony *Mary* Moreau. On a whim I went to see how many women named Mary might live in Howard Hall nearby where I live on campus. Outside the door by the phone, was a list of names and phone numbers. Of some one hundred and seventy-six student residents I found many beautiful names, such as Grace, Juanita, Rosalind, Melani, Vanessa, Stephanie, Patrice, Laura, Burgandie, Dawn, Ashley, Carrie, Leticia, Jacqueline, Andria, Jill, Nicole, Christina, Amina, Holly, Marina, Heather, Alicia, Alyssa, Yasemin, Kimberly, Kiersten, Camille, Melissa, Lindsay, Sonja, and Lina. There was but one woman named Mary. And indeed there always remains one woman named Mary, holy Mary, mother of God, whose name I pray we shall never forget, and whom I hope, whatever our own name, we shall all call upon to "pray for us sinners now and at the hour of our death."

Saint Joseph

NEARBY OLD COLLEGE and the Log Chapel a memorial to the original founders of Notre Dame has been raised along the sidewalk north of the Architecture Building.[6] An imposing statue of an older Saint Joseph stands atop the stone monument, and a child Jesus, no longer a baby, is held up in his strong arms. Saint Joseph stands there so impressive and so solid. Joseph stands for reliable. He kept his word; he kept his promises. You know you can count on Joseph. If integrity is what you seek, Joseph should be your patron saint.

As is traditional, this Saint Joseph is sculpted with a lily in his right hand. Joseph guarded the virginity of Mary, his spouse, and the mother of Our Lord Jesus Christ. He must have been a man of chaste integrity in his own body and a man of modesty. While I was writing these words, Wendy Shalit, a recent graduate of Williams College, where the best and the brightest receive a superlative education, spoke on campus about the virtue of modesty. She urged young women and young men to reclaim their heritage from an era when the human body was better protected and held more sacred. When taunted that she was prudish and was not comfortable

6. After the magnificent renovation of the old university library, the Architecture Building is now called Bond Hall.

with her body, she responds that she is very comfortable with her body but not comfortable with the bodies of others up against hers. When taunted that her message is that of a repressed woman closed in upon her modesty, she replies that she treasures her body. All the more reason why she wants to preserve it intact for someone to whom she would give herself because they respect her and know the unique value of her person that gives heart and worth to her body. The prudish and the promiscuous both say they cannot be "touched." Modest persons say they can be touched, but wait to be touched by someone who will cherish them forever. Saint Joseph would be an example and a patron saint of modesty—modesty of body and of soul, a man for others, reliable and wholesome, a human being with a love to die for.

Saint Joseph looks out across Saint Mary's Lake to Columba Hall, the residence of the brothers of Holy Cross on the campus. Father Sorin built Notre Dame with his heart and his head, but the small band of brothers who accompanied him built up the stones with their bare hands. Life was not easy over the years for these first pioneers in the wilderness of Indiana. Attached to Columba Hall is a small building at the east end, which served as the campus infirmary. There is an air space separating the residence in order to secure a quarantine for the sick who suffered from epidemic illness in those early days. Yellow fever, in particular, ran through the Holy Cross community. Neither the young nor the old were spared. Malaria was also a bane for the early Notre Dame, much as it remains a plague that sickens or kills millions of people around the world each year to this day. Only when Father Sorin had the swampland between the two lakes drained and filled did the community begin to be delivered from malarial illness. The so-called *kranken-haus* (the infirmary) in more recent years became the Solitude of Saint Joseph, a house of prayer and a place of spiritual retreat. I see Saint Joseph on his pedestal looking across the lake at that whole scene, and I think the perennial illness of us all remains our mortality, and the only cure that we need for our life and death is the promise of grace and the hope of resurrection given us in the love of the child Jesus whom Joseph held in his arms, and who would grow to manhood and give up his life for us on the cross on Calvary Hill.

Sacred Heart

IN THE CENTER of the quadrangle in front of the Dome Building, which once was the entire University of Notre Dame complete with dining halls and dormitories, classrooms and offices, there stands a lone statue of the Sacred Heart on a small granite pedestal. Jesus looks out upon the French Provincial architecture some fifty yards away, which was built up from the ruins in one summer after a devastating fire had devastated the whole university. Once more it has been rebuilt, but this day from the inside and because of the destruction of age rather than fire. The Main Building has been completely renovated and restored to its original splendor and a further elegance. Even the roundelay encircling the outside of the quadrangle has been rebuilt and the pattern of the original heart shape can be seen clearly in the brickwork that edges the pavement. In a circular walkway at the very center of the quad there stands the statue of Jesus, whose Sacred Heart of love remains visible at the center of the heart of the university. His arms are outstretched, and carved in the pedestal are the Latin words *Venite ad me omnes* (come to me all). If one finishes the biblical quotation from which these four words were taken, it reads: "Come to me all you who are weary and are carrying heaven burdens, and I will give you rest. Take my yoke upon you, and learn from me; for I am gentle and humble in heart, and you will find rest for your souls. For my yoke is easy, and my burden is light" (Mt 11:28–30). The unconditional love of Jesus is symbolized in his heart depicted with a crown of thorns, which reminds us that "no one has greater love than this to lay down one's life for one's friends" (Jn 15:13). In a windstorm some time ago a branch fell from a maple tree and knocked the statue off its pedestal. Jesus fell head first into the ground. The cast iron statute was not damaged, only embarrassed. I came by to see the debacle just as a young man had seized the rare moment to jump up upon the empty pedestal and pose, arms outstretched, for a picture taken adoringly by his girlfriend at his feet.

Restored to his pedestal, Jesus looks upon the Dome. His mother Mary shines there in solitary golden splendor. People wonder how they ever put that enormous and heavy statue of Our Lady on the top of the golden Dome without benefit of crane or modern machinery. Raising her must have been an assumption into heaven. I think they must have built a cupola on top of the Dome, attached a hook to its ceiling, and with a block and tackle raised the statue of the Blessed Virgin Mary into the cupola. A floor was then constructed under her feet and the cupola was torn down. Our Lady to this day stands and overlooks the entire campus of Notre Dame.

I wonder if she is ever lonely all alone on top of our world. I often wish we had a statue of Mary and Joseph with their arms around each other. I own an icon of Mary's marriage betrothal with Joseph. She is shown running out of her house with her cape flying behind her and bounding into the arms of Joseph who is coming out of his house. Over them both flies a banner in the wind, reminiscent of these words from the King James version of the Song of Songs: "And his banner over me was love" (2:4).

I wonder if the heart of Jesus is ever lonely all alone with outstretched arms eager to receive the troubles and burdens of everyone else who comes along. Of course, I know Jesus is the beloved of the Father and enfolded in the Trinity with love beyond our comprehension. And I know Mary is the bride of the Holy Spirit and enfolded in this same love of the Father and the Son. And so are we all: "As the Father has loved me, so I have loved you; abide in my love" (Jn 15:9). Nonetheless, when I am lonely, praying my rosary on the quad under the Dome in the night and no one is around, I stand before Jesus with his arms outstretched and facing his mother standing alone on the Dome, and I can imagine him saying, "If you lean forward, my dear, I would hold you up before you fall."

Corby at Gettysburg

IN FRONT OF Corby Hall, which is attached to the Basilica, stands a statue of Father William Corby, C.S.C., giving sacramental absolution to the Union troops at the dawn of the Civil War battle of Gettysburg. General absolution was given to all the soldiers attentive to his prayer. They were in danger of death, and God's mercy was not to be impeded by anything requiring time when there was no time. His hand is raised in a blessing. So many of them were about to meet their God before night would fall. The original statue stands at the memorial battlefield in Pennsylvania, where thousands of visitors come in memory of those fallen soldiers from the North and from the South who here gave their lives in a bloody war between brother states. Fifty thousand deaths in a battle that should never have been fought equal all the U.S. casualties suffered by this country in the Vietnam War in a land far away against an enemy all unknown to us. That battle should also never have been fought, had we only known how to make peace.

I imagine there was a chaplain on the side of the South who blessed the troops and gave them hope of God's mercy. God takes no sides in our warfare. There may be such a thing as a just war, but one wonders if the good is ever wholly on one side. Such are the bitter conflicts of human life and such the endless ambiguities of our judgment. In John's gospel when Andrew and Simon are called to be disciples, they ask Jesus where he dwells. And Jesus tells them "Come and see" (Jn 2:39). Much later in the same gospel Jesus goes to his friend Lazarus who has died. He asks where they have laid him, and they say to Jesus with the same words in the gospel Greek, "Come and see" (Jn 11:34). And Jesus wept.

Jesus proclaims to us: come and see where God ever dwells in light and in life. We proclaim to Jesus: come and see where human beings end dwelling in dark and in death. Father Corby sent the soldiers into the mortal conflict with a blessing, for the day was dismal. Jesus calls us to come and see where we are destined by God to dwell with him in the resurrection of the body and life everlasting. For the first time in John's gospel, Jesus, at the tomb of Lazarus, encounters death. The smell of decay issues from the tomb, and the family is afraid to roll back the rock. Lazarus is resuscitated by Jesus and brought back to this life, where he will some day die again. In the resurrection of Jesus from the tomb he walks right through the rock, which is rolled back not to let him escape but to let the women see that he is not there. Death has no power over him, and Jesus does not dwell where we come to dwell without him.

Abraham Lincoln said that "no house divided against itself can stand," and he took his text from the Gospel of Matthew (12:25). Jesus prayed, "As you, Father, are in me and I am in you, may they also be in us, so that the world may believe that you have sent me. The glory that you have given me I have given them, so that they may be one, as we are one" (Jn 17:21–22). Long after the battle of Gettysburg and long after two bloody world wars, humanity knows now as never before that we must have one world. We are spaceship Earth, and our divisions and death-dealing conflicts must cease if we are to survive. For those of us with faith in the Lord of mercy we constitute the body of Christ, crucified with him but alive with the hope of glory and the love of all God's children, who are our brothers and our sisters. There remains only one Lord, one God, one Father of us all, who has called us into existence with Jesus, God-with-us, who promised us that the glory the Father has given him will be given to us all. The statue of Father Corby tells the story of Lazarus in the human condition. The statue of the Sacred Heart in the Dome quadrangle nearby tells the story of Jesus in the divine condition to which we are invited as Nathaniel was. Come and see!

The Woman at the Well

ON THE WEST side of O'Shaughnessy Hall, a configuration of life-sized bronze sculptures anchor a semicircular cove of wooden benches and stone steps. In the center of these sculptures the Samaritan woman at the well draws all eyes. The sculpture itself is one of the masterpieces of Ivan Mestrovic, the resident artist in the O'Shaughnessy art gallery when the building was inaugurated. She is standing on one side of the marble well while hugging a stone water jug to her body. Jesus is seated on the rim of the well on the opposite side, and he appears magisterial. His divinity would not be hard to believe in his pose of majesty and authority. Her sensuality and flesh would not be hard to believe from the sensuous pose of her body in its curvaceous and yielding stance. The s-curve of her spine and the definition of her buttocks says enough about her five husbands.[7] She represents more than the Samaritan woman, of course. She stands for unfaithful Israel and her many lovers taking the place of the God whose loving covenant with her was made forever. She stands for the human soul, whose femininity is so often overlooked and abused. She stands for us, women and men, who seek day after day waters that slake not our thirst. Like this woman, static in a moment

7. See the story in John's gospel (chapter 4).

of time, we need to hear the eternal word of God in our hearts saying, "The water that I will give will become in them a spring of water gushing up to eternal life" (Jn 4:14).

In the Book of Ezekiel we read of the Lord God's love for Israel:

> You grew up and became tall and arrived at full womanhood; your breasts were formed, and your hair had grown; yet you were naked and bare. I passed by you again and looked on you; you were at the age for love. I spread the edge of my cloak over you, and covered your nakedness: I pledged myself to you and entered into a covenant with you, says the Lord God, and you became mine. Then I bathed you with water and washed off the blood from you, and anointed you with oil. I clothed you with embroidered cloth and with sandals of fine leather; I bound you in fine linen and covered you with rich fabric. I adorned you with ornaments: I put bracelets on your arms, a chain on your neck, a ring on your nose, earrings in your ears, and a beautiful crown upon your head. You were adorned with gold and silver, while your clothing was of fine linen, rich fabric, and embroidered cloth. You had choice flour and honey and oil for food. You grew exceedingly beautiful, fit to be a queen. Your fame spread among the nations on account of your beauty, for it was perfect because of my splendor that I had bestowed on you, says the Lord God. But you trusted in your beauty, and played the whore because of your fame, and lavished your whorings on any passer-by. (16:7–15)

When I read this passage with my mind's eye on the woman at the well, I want to cry. God has loved each one of us so well, and our response is so unaware and so reluctant. I see the embarrassment of the woman at the well. I feel the embarrassment that women might feel when their sensuality is singled out as the problem in this whole scene. The body, however, is not the enemy of God. It is the human heart that is the problem. The bronze sculptures far to either side of the woman at the well depict a male thinker and a male scribe. It is the heart and soul of us all that is unfaithful. The body is all too innocent, and we identify women with the body and men with the mind all too quickly. Sin is in our will. The flesh is the victim of our abuse. That is why Jesus treats this woman with such compassion and respect. He neither scolds her nor blames her. He invites her to seek the fountain of living waters within herself which he will make flow in her like an everlasting spring. And her body and soul hear him. She leaves the jug that she is hugging in her arms and which represents her habitual way of coping with the thirsts of unhappiness in the human soul. Unprovided now, she goes to the town as an apostle to tell her people that she has met in Jesus the Messiah of God. Like Mary Magdalene at the tomb she recognizes her Lord, and she becomes an apostle. It would take humility on our part to be evangelized by our own body and its innocence, by our own soul and its womanliness. She receives the word of God, but not in passivity. In the end she leaves everything to give her life for what she has been given. And we have been given so much, and leave behind us so little. We hug our empty jugs that hold so little water. I never sit in this enclosure and look upon the woman at the well without an awareness that I am her and she is me.

Moses

ON THE WEST side of the Memorial Library a larger-than-life bronze statue of Moses dominates the walkway to the side entrance. With one foot on the golden calf flattened to the ground face up and one arm raised with index finger pointing skyward and dramatically proclaiming there is but the one and only God, the figure of Moses is awesome. The sculpture is the work of a student or disciple of Ivan Mestrovic, the Croation artist whose magnificent marble pietà in the Basilica is worthy of comparison with Michelangelo's *Pieta* in St. Peter's Basilica in Rome. Coed students paint the toenails of Moses with nail polish. I think it is the coed students, for they would more likely have the wherewithal. At first I was disturbed at the defacing of a serious work of art. But the nail polish weathers off. I can hear a giggle and a voice in the night saying, "hey, Moses, you got to lighten up." And I smile.

The upraised index finger of this impressive Moses reminds me of the students who wave their hand and index finger in unison at our football games. They chant "we are number one." They chant "we are N.D." On the roof of the thirteen-story Grace Hall that looms over the shoulder of the statue of Moses, the students erect a large electric sign proclaiming to all who come near the university "we are number 1." That sign had not been lit for quite some time when in 1993 Notre Dame defeated Florida State University, who all season long had been the top-ranked team in the football polls. Now Notre Dame was a safe bet for the college national championship. Now we could illumine the sign, and wave our finger in the air with an air of truth. We were number one.

Our elation would last but one week. On a day that will be remembered forever in sadness, Boston College defeated a miraculous comeback effort by a Notre Dame team that in the last minutes retook the game. In the last seconds a field goal kick turned the game around in a miraculous way yet a second time, and that day and that football season were forever darkened. I can say that I have never recovered, for I thought God intended us to win that come-from-behind unthinkable victory, and then in an instant it was taken away. Lots of idols here, and Moses would understand the people needed something tangible. I know I did. We celebrated too soon, presumed too much, thought too little of the other team. And let who may say, "hey, fella, lighten up."

On the night of the Florida State victory the week before this dark afternoon, there was a darker night. Students celebrating the victory with food and drink and driving back to campus encountered another group of students who had celebrated as well. They had no car, could find no cab, and were walking with the traffic along a two-lane road on a dark night. The car hit a young first-year student, a woman from Lewis Hall. Maura Fox died instantly. The car did not stop. Neither the driver nor the passengers claim to know exactly what happened, for it all happened so fast and in darkness. But nothing in the lives of all involved would ever be the same. The rector of Lewis Hall erected a memorial sign by the road, and at times I see fresh flowers placed lovingly on that marker. And Sister Kathleen was mad, mad like the mothers against drunk drivers (MADD) are mad when one of their very own children is killed on the road. To what extent alcohol was a factor in this accident was never proven in a court of law, and the truth may never be known. We know no one meant harm. We know these things happen. We know whether we are responsible for an accident or innocent of an accident. We always will know that we did it. The pain does not go away for all involved. Yes, we are N.D., and yes, we may be number one. But in the quiet of the night, all of us must also say, "I am so-and-so, and I do such-and such." Maybe Moses should lighten up and maybe he should not. And yes indeed there is but one and only one God to whom we all belong as God's beloved children—whoever we are, whatever we do.

Between the first and second draft of this short meditation, the women's basketball team won the 2001 national championship. How strange are the humble ways of redemption. I think it is time to forget Florida State and time to forgive, beginning with ourselves. We are not all bad. We are not all good. And we are Notre Dame.

Saint Ann

IN THE BACK of Corby Hall where the priests and brothers of Holy Cross have their meals together, there is a patio that opens out to the lawn on the edge of the Grotto to the north. The president used to park his car in that niche, but one day it was turned into a small courtyard. Trees were planted, bushes and flowers of every kind tended. Outdoor furniture appeared. I sit there often with coffee in the morning, or a beer in the evening which I discreetly sip from a cola cup with a lid. It has become a sacred place, for I pray there while I watch the clouds go by, or I study the endless activity around the walnut trees that dominate the lawn on the outside of the patio. Birds, squirrels, chipmunks, passersby, and traffic to the Basilica sacristy right around the corner come and go. I feed the birds and the chipmunks peanuts, and they become tame. Saint Francis had the creatures of the earth eating out of his hand, and I suspect his secret was peanuts. The bird omens that came to the waiting sibyls of antiquity must have been encouraged by a peanut in either hand. The brick walls around the patio were recently scrubbed clean with acid and water. They shine bright yellow in the sun, a flat tan in the shade, and in the half light of dawn or of dusk a shadowy off-yellow. In the dim light the texture of the brick suddenly emerges. The walls are not flat at all. There are shadows everywhere from the bricks in jagged formation. Nothing is quite what it appears when one sits in a patio and stares long at what truly exists.

On one side of the patio there is a limestone sculpture of Saint Ann seated with the child Mary at her knee. Saint Ann has a radiant and peaceful smile. She has the joy of a mother exulting in her child's existence and in her desire to instruct her in every good way. Mary is depicted as a little adult, and she has a slight scowl on her face. It was never easy to be little. The sculpture is weathered and in style appears to date from the medieval period. I think it is an original, probably from an abandoned monastery, and on loan to Corby Hall from the Snite Museum at Notre Dame.

Everything good came from an antecedent that is good. Creation was found to be good because God is good. Mary was a special creation of God, and her mother must have been good. Saint Ann, in turn, must have known the goodness of her parents. And so forth back to the beginning, back to the twinkle in God's eye in the beginning. "Let there be light." God is in us all, or more accurately, we are all in God. Tennyson's poem "Flower in the Crannied Wall" says it so simply: "Little Flower—but *if* I could understand/What you are, root and all, and all in all,/I should know what God and man is." The genealogy of Jesus given in Matthew and in Luke includes very ordinary people, even sinful people. The so-called shady ladies in the otherwise male genealogy of Matthew have given marginal people hope that their lives also count. Rahab was the prostitute who saved the lives of the Israelite spies who reconnoitered the promised land. Bathsheba was the woman David seduced, and whose son would succeed to the throne as King Solomon. Tamar and Ruth both were rejected by misfortune, but they contrived by strong desire and native wit to enable themselves to bear children, who in God's providence proved to be the ancestors of Our Lord Jesus Christ. We all have a role to play, and no man or woman is an island, not Jesus of Nazareth, not Mary his mother, not Saint Ann her mother, not you, not I.

I was standing in front of Saint Ann and admiring her smile when I looked at the base of this less-than-life-size sculpture. Hidden in the vegetation at her feet was a duck's nest with three eggs the size of chicken eggs. On the following days I watched the mother duck in perfect camouflage sitting on the eggs. Day after day I came in eager anticipation that perhaps I would see ducklings. At the last I saw an abandoned nest and smashed eggs, with orange yoke running over the stones. Had a squirrel or a raccoon discovered the nest when the mother was absent? Had a crow or a jay invaded the nest and broken the eggs when they discovered them unprotected? Life is not fair, I thought. Lots of eggs don't make it. Why anything? Why anybody? Most of all, why me? And through it all, I knew, Saint Ann yet sits with Mary at her knee, for the emergent world remains God's egg in God's care, and the Easter mystery is not just for children to discover in the grass.

Saint Edward

ON THE LAWN in front of Saint Edward's Hall stands a large statue of Saint Edward, patron saint of Edward Sorin, founder in 1842 of the University of Notre Dame. Edward was king of England in medieval times, and during his reign he was a protector of the Church. The statue shows him with the Basilica of the Sacred Heart in his arms. Edward Sorin likewise protected the Church in the building of this school, where learning would both enhance the understanding of the Church and defend it against misunderstanding in the popular judgment of this country.

When Jesus stood before the power of Pontius Pilate to condemn him to death, he called upon no heavenly army to save him. To Peter in the Garden of Gethsemane he confided that his Father could send legions of angels to his rescue, but that his kingdom was not of this world. Religion and Church have no armies in their own name. They depend for their earthly welfare upon the human community, upon the protection of the state, upon the fairness of reason that should not impose belief upon anyone nor impede the practice of religion to anyone. When all is said and done, we depend upon God.

Our heroes, whether they are compared with Jesus who died for love of us or a Socrates who died for love of the truth, are always vulnerable to the will of the majority or the will of those in power. *Might makes right* is the law of this world all too often. If one counts all the persecutions of Christians in this century in places where freedom of religion has been abolished, the cloud of witnesses may well surpass all previous centuries combined. As I am writing this, a blood bath in East Timor decimates the Catholic population. Muslim countries have not been favorable to other religions, and in fairness it should be said neither had Christian Europe in many past centuries. The more one believes in the pure truth, the more one is tempted to impose that truth on others willing or not. It is a sad commentary on human nature that our religious wars pit the very best of our devotion against other human beings equally but differently devoted. The statue of Saint Edward protecting the Church is not just about England, nor just about Father Sorin as guardian of Notre Dame; it is also about freedom of religion that is a human right owned by every human being and a blessings to be protected by any government. We are blessed in this country to enjoy freedom of religion with a promise that no state religion shall be established lest we be tempted to impede freedom of conscience.

Dante needed the guidance of Vergil to reach the heavenly presence of Beatrice. Faith needs the assistance of reason to establish its own realm. Catholic theology needs the thinking of the university if it is to develop its beauty and avoid its diminishments. The Church needs the protection of the world if it is to flourish.

A friend of mine was a mountain climber and cross-country hiker of considerable stamina. Living with us was a brave and energetic little dog, a descendant of the wild dingoes of Australia. The dog always wanted to go along for the adventure, and Jim finally allowed the dog to come. But long into the trail the dog lay down with exhaustion and would not move. When Jim walked home at the end of the day he was carrying the spent dog in his arms like a lamb. Saint Edward with the Church in his arms is a reflection of Jesus, the good shepherd, with the tired and lost sheep in his arms. We need power that is loving, and love that is powerful. Saint Edwards of the world, pray for us.

Orestes Brownson

IN THE CRYPT of the Basilica of the Sacred Heart lies the body of a great homemade intellectual of nineteenth-century America and a convert to the Catholic faith. He would serve the Church as writer and spokesman of national acclaim for thirty years. He was called the John Henry Newman of the United States of America. Orestes Brownson was born a Yankee, a self-educated man, an Emersonian self-reliant man, a mountain man from Vermont. He had the strengths and the weaknesses that went along with independence from tradition. His mind was not tutored by a fully balanced education in a university, and his mind was not restrained by situations that he would come to see with prejudice. Before Marx wrote of the plight of the worker in the industrial world, Orestes Brownson (1803–1876) had lamented the same injustices in the pages of his *Boston Quarterly Review*. After his conversion to Roman Catholicism, he wrote extensively and edited some twenty volumes of the *Brownson Quarterly Review*, a magazine of national reputation that reached by mail into the homes of rural America where most of the population of this country dwelt.

His conversion to the Catholic faith was not sudden. Just as Newman made a long journey of study through the centuries of Christian tradition until he found his way to Rome, so Brownson made a long journey of allegiance to one religion after the other, including one of his own, until at the last he found his way into the Catholic Church in 1844.

His grave marker is a marble slab set into the middle of the main isle of the Basilica crypt, which was once called the Brownson Memorial Chapel. I have never seen anyone walk over his grave, yet I suspect he lies there all unknown. A small plaque at the back of the crypt does tell his story, but it is tucked almost out of sight. The Latin on his tombstone reads: "Here lies Orestes A. Brownson, who humbly acknowledged the true faith and lived a life of integrity. With tongue and pen he firmly defended both Church and country. Though his body lies in death, the work of his mind endures—immortal monuments of his genius."

Brownson left a request that he be buried at Notre Dame, and his body was brought from Detroit to the crypt chapel in 1886, some ten years after his death. Only John Cardinal O'Hara, C.S.C., enjoys that same privilege of burial within the Basilica. Brownson was a man of the mind and a man of the Church, and he must have thought that in some preeminent way the Church did its thinking at Notre Dame. The centrality of Notre Dame even then in the nineteenth century and surely today lies in its central location within the United States. If a national Catholic university were to emerge, it would not be connected with a major city that would tend to lend it regional prominence at the expense of national loyalty. If a national Catholic university were to emerge, it would need the loyalty of its alumni and alumnae. That loyalty is best nurtured by a residential campus that creates its own family and its own world in a location where little centrifugal force is felt from the environs. Notre Dame is just such a place, a world of Catholic faith that has been described as the world's largest seminary, for it does sow seeds of Christian life in its inhabitants who cross paths so often and so intimately in four years of communal residence and Catholic education. That Brownson would make his last statement at Notre Dame in his choice of the place where he would lie until the day of judgment says much of him as a son of the Church and of the University of Notre Dame as a spiritual work of providence.

Saint Jude

JUST WEST OF the nave of the Basilica and south of the barred windows that guard the gold and silver chalice treasure trove in the sacristy museum there stands a statue of Saint Jude. A small circular concrete platform is flanked by two benches. Tucked on the lawn between Corby Hall and the Basilica, this space is a quiet spot where mothers with small children might find a place out of the traffic. Most people assume the male figure must be Saint Joseph, but here stands Saint Jude, the patron of lost causes, the patron of people in desperate need and in despair. Jude (also named Thaddeus) was one of the twelve apostles of Jesus, and how he became the popular patron of hopeless causes is shrouded in mystery, as is so much of the devotion to the saints. Their stories tell us not so much what happened in proven history as they tell us what the people of God needed and what they expected and hoped for from their patron saints and from their God. I found a prayer to Saint Jude that says it well:

> O God, through your Blessed Saint Jude, I pray for help in my extreme need. The despair I feel has blocked out all hope, all confidence, all faith in a just solution to this situation. Bring to me a spirit of trust and an optimistic attitude which will bring about an improvement in my circumstances. You know all my needs and so I pray for

> speedy assistance, along with a restoration of my knowledge that all things work for good when trust in you mercy is placed above all other thoughts.[8]

In the revelations of Juliana of Norwich, she tells of God's promise to her: "Sin is necessary, but all will be well, and all will be well, and every kind of thing will be well."[9] When she wondered how God could make everything well, she was told that though such an outcome would be impossible for us to secure, for God nothing was impossible. God can write straight with crooked lines. Even sin serves. In the gospel, Elizabeth says to Mary, "And blessed is she who believed that there would be a fulfillment of what was spoken to her by the Lord" (Lk 1:45). And to a doubting Thomas, Jesus says, "Blessed are those who have not seen and yet have come to believe" (Jn 20:29).

In the creed we affirm that Jesus will come to judge the living and the dead and of his kingdom there will be no end. The early Christians did not dread that coming as if it were a day of judgment and wrath. They were eager for the second coming of Jesus Christ, just as the whole world awaited so long the coming of the Messiah of God in the birth of Mary's child in Bethlehem. "Come, Lord Jesus!" is how the Christian scriptures conclude, and it is a joyful cry of hope. In our imagination we think of God's final judgment as a

8. Ann Ball, *A Litany of Saints* (Huntington, Ind.: Our Sunday Visitor Press, 1993), 142–43.

9. Julian of Norwich, *Showings*, trans. Edmund Colledge and James Walsh (New York: Paulist Press, 1978), Thirteenth Revelation (long text), 225.

kind of final examination. One is called before the bench, and the judge presents evidence against you. Our experience of bench judgment is one of fear, for we know judges cannot know the whole circumstance and they are not always fair or well informed. That is our experience of judgment in this life, and we unfairly project that image of judgment upon Jesus our savior, who is far more wise and far more merciful than we are.

Even given a judgment none should fear, I do not believe the second coming is about the revelation of what we have done in our lives, but rather the revelation of all that God has accomplished in and through us for the salvation of all peoples. The last judgment will be the justification of the ways of God to man. The second coming will be the reversal of the tapestry of this world's history in which we saw but the backside, where threads of gold and threads of black did seem to conflict and comprise nothing we could comprehend. But now, when we see the whole picture with God's eyes, we look upon a masterpiece of beauty and love that God has created, shaped, loved, and judged now to be finished and complete. The University of Notre Dame will be a figure in that tapestry of the kingdom of God come at last to its eternal home. Its blue and gold threads will weave its people together in the common endeavor to know and love the living God. And the mother of Jesus, Notre Dame, will be loved for all the ways by her intercession and prayers with us she has entwined in our lives the hidden graces of God.